Go Dream: A DIY Guide to Dream Interpretation

Mark Birch-Machin PhD

Freedom Publishing Limited
12 Dukes Court, Bognor Road
Chichester. PO19 8FX, United Kingdom
www.freedompublishing.net

ISBN: 978-1-908154-54-5

British Library Cataloguing in Publication Data. A catalogue record for this book is available from the British Library

Typesetting by Avocet Typeset, Bideford, Devon, EX39 2BP
Printed and bound in the UK

Table of Contents

Dedication

This book is dedicated to:
The one whose name is like flowing oil, the kindest one I know
"While I sleep my heart is awake"

What Others Are Saying About This Book

"Dreams are such a part of God's design for us and his way of speaking of his love and purpose to us. Mark has written a fantastic guide to dreams and their interpretation to help us understand the mysteries of dreams and to understand the voice of our creator who knows and loves us intimately. Additional to being a respected and award-winning scientist, Mark has always been down to earth and relational and appeals to those who want to know more about this subject. Whether you are a regular dreamer or someone like me who often forgets their dreams but occasionally remembers a significant "non pizza" dream, then this book is for you! In fact, it is a relief to know that there is help to understand a complex and often daunting subject. Get ready to grow, learn, be activated and to bless many!"

Kate Smith,
President, Catch the Fire World
Senior Leader, Catch the Fire Raleigh-Durham, USA

Mark is a remarkable man with many diverse and awe-inspiring Godly gifts. This book will equip you in ways you never thought possible. Mark lives this book! He carries revelation with ease and interprets dreams in all life circumstances! I love his gentle humility, his fun-loving spirit and his wisdom in difficult circumstances. Mark's love of Jesus and his ability to host the presence of God without pollution or dilution is astonishing. Time spent with Mark is time well spent and so as you let Mark speak into your life through this book, you won't be disappointed. You will come away from it richer, as I do every time I'm with him.

Emma Stark,
Director, Global Prophetic Alliance and
Glasgow Prophetic Centre
Core Leader, British Isles Council of Prophets
Author of *The Prophetic Warrior*

"The most significant turning point in my life came through a dream when the Lord Jesus came to me and affirmed in me his Word. It changed my life forever; I saw angels, Heavenly incense and extraordinary sights. I only understood what I saw because Jesus explained it all to me. But I suspect that if this book had been available, it would have opened up to me some of the mysteries in that dream encounter with Jesus. Mark is a Seer to whom God has given an unusual but profoundly insightful prophetic ministry. If you're a dreamer, this book promises to give a 360° perspective on some of the imagery you will encounter."

Yinka Oyekan,
President of the Baptist Union of Great Britain
Senior Minister, The Gate, Reading UK

"I have had the privilege of joining Mark and others doing dream interpretation in a restaurant in New York to patrons of the restaurant. It was so fun to help them connect the dots of their dream into a storyline of the Father's love for them. The teaching that Mark provides in dream interpretation is so simple and doable that it takes all the fear out of sharing the gospel using dream interpretation. Enjoy the tools provided in this book as you explore God's love language towards you personally and help the world around you connect to the Lord!"

Tammi White,
Pastor, Life Center Church, New York, USA

"With profound pleasure I commend Prof. Mark Birch-Machin PhD and his new book on dreams, having learned so very much from both his teaching and friendship. He presents the interpretive process practically and with great clarity. This piece of work is sharp, like an arrow, correctly aligned, full of direction, overflowing with the creative force of the Holy Spirit. Through it, Mark demonstrates for us one of the many different expressions of how a prophet moves and works in the world today. Gone are the days of the lone voice, standing suited and booted, giving static lectures. This book is an invitation into the interactive journey of listening to God. Prof. Mark has the extraordinary combination of being both a Scientist and a Creative. He's an expert in both, with an ability to put into words exactly what he sees and encounters, teaching and guiding us in the process. Warm and approachable, Mark moves powerfully in the prophetic world. God is using this book to expand and accelerate our understanding of the Secrets of God."

Rebecca King,
Founder & Director Invictus Prophetic Network
Core Leader, British Isles Council of Prophets

"I have had the privilege of knowing Mark for over 10 years. I've seen how he has grown in his love for his Heavenly Father and the joy of the Lord. I've seen an incredible transformation in his life, a reflection of the transforming power that is at work in him. This book, following on from his *Speakers of Life* book, has incredible revelation and insight that have come through Mark spending hours in the presence of God, listening and following Holy Spirit. This book has amazing depth and rich insight into understanding dreams and visions. The result is a book that will refresh you, that will help deliver your own personal revelation with wisdom and understanding. I would highly recommend this book, and would recommend when you read it that you journey through it with the Holy Spirit as your guide, with an open heart and an open mindset to understand more of what your Heavenly Father wants to release to you."

Alan Dickinson,
Very Reverend of the Order of Saint Leonard
Senior Apostolic Leader, AsOne NorthEast, UK

"If you are a looking for a practical manual on how to interpret dreams in both the faith based and secular areas, look no further than this book by Professor Mark Birch-Machin. This book expands the work of his first book and allows the reader to dive deeper in the biblical interpretation of dreams that takes you far beyond a list of biblical symbols that you can find on a Google search. This book will help you to dive deeper into living a prophetic lifestyle while understanding the practical matters of how our physical body works as it relates to sleep. As you read this book, get ready to go deeper in your relationship with God as you explore God's revelation given as you sleep!"

LaTasha Robinson,
Founder of BARN Prophetic Ministries, Paris, France
Author of the Prophetic Processing Toolkit

"Mark is a practitioner and shepherd, desiring all of us to live in clarity with the dreams God gives us. In this book we take a deep dive not only into dream interpretation tools, but also into understanding dream categories, how dreams relate to our sleep, and how God is loving and relating to us through our dreams. This is a must read if you have questions about your dreams, or if you need practical guidance about how to dream, or if you want to understand the way God communicates to you as you dream."

Meg Saunders,
Former Senior Advisor, Office of the Chaplain, US Senate
Missionary Pastor and Leader in Washington DC, USA

"If you are looking for practical wisdom on the subject of dreams and dream interpretation, you've found it with Go Dream. There is unique treasure to be mined in our dreams, and I would invite you to dive into the beautiful mysteries that they hold. Mark's perspective, experience, and expertise make him a powerful voice to have as your dream mentor. The investment of the practical followed by the invitation into the 'Divine Love Story' is such an incredible truth of the intimate language of dreams. This book will become an incredibly valuable resource to your library and to your life."

Ben Armstrong,
Prophetic Ministry Director, Bethel Church, Redding CA

Acknowledgements

Those who know me will tell you that I am all about team and so I have great pleasure in declaring that this book in your hand would never have been lived and written without the reality and benefit of team in my life. First and foremost, I am extremely grateful to my family team; Juliet, my wife of thirty-six years, and our two adult sons Joel and Sam. I am continually inspired and deeply grateful that we are a family of faith and of fun; where we encourage each other to fly higher whilst ensuring that we do not take ourselves too seriously. Thank you to my parents, Roy and Irene for their continual encouragement and love throughout my life.

There is such a large team of people I would like to thank but I'm sure you would like to start reading the book before page 100 so here is a tip of the iceberg thank you list. Thanks to those 'sold out lovers of God' who have provided written endorsements of this book. Thank you to the amazing prayer team who in their busy lives find the time to provide me with daily prayer cover. You are Karen Vickers, Lisa 'amigo' Gowland, Natasha Tyrwhitt-Drake, Claire McCourt, Rachel Elliot-Downing, David Vickers and Sandy Dirks. Thanks to the Speakers Of Life (SOL) core team and the original seven members that God has grown from our Friday night prophetic gatherings in our converted garage to a network connected with approximately 300+ churches globally. In this context, I would like to mention Anna Spencer, Tim Lozinski, Holly Craigs, Juliet Birch-Machin, Leah Harris, Lisa 'amigo' Gowland, Natasha Tyrwhitt-Drake, Rachel Elliot-Downing, David and Karen Vickers, Sola and Liz Idowu.

Thank you to the wonderful SOL prophetic appointments team

and the SOL network family, you are a living global family where we all own a piece of SOL; we are from the same 'tribe' as we come together under the name of Jesus. Thank you to the "4", that together we burn greater with the fire and passion of God and his Kingdom; you are Paul, Alan, David and myself. Thank you, Paul, for pushing me to do "10 more reps" in the spirit realm (and for your Vlogs which helped to inspire aspects of this book), to Alan for encouraging me to fly higher and further and to David for modelling the love of Jesus so well.

Thanks to the friendship and help over the last 11 years from the Glasgow Prophetic Centre team, particularly Emma and David Stark, Sarah-Jane Biggart and Sam Robertson. Thanks also to the encouragement of my new friends at the British Isles Council of Prophets, I am loving being part of the team and the journey. Thanks to my wife Juliet and Steve Abley for being the first people in my University student days to tell me about Jesus and how to have a living relationship with Him. In addition, thank you to Steve Stotesbury for interceding for me during the time of decision leading to the acceptance of Jesus into my life.

Thanks to all the encouragement from The Bay Church (Whitley Bay, UK), 'The Family' in Byker, Andy and Judith Acreman and my Essex friends, Minty, Julia and Jason Powell and the Northern Prophetic School of Supernatural Ministry gang, Ceri and Jonathan Davies and all my River Church friends, and my extended Christian families in Washington DC, New York (Life Center Church), New Jersey, Paris, Sydney and Adelaide.

Thank you to our many friends at Catch the Fire, particularly for the encouragement of John Arnott (who inspired me to start the Speakers of Life network), Duncan and Kate Smith and Mary Audrey Raycroft. Thank you to those who have championed this book (and other books) in me from the start and continue to do so; particular mention should go to Claire, Annalisa, 'Amigo' and Sam and Jenny 'from Jersey'. Thanks to my wife Juliet, Holly Craigs and Natasha Tyrwhitt-Drake for proof reading the final draft of the Chapters. Thanks to the those who have allowed their dreams to be used as public examples to help us all learn more about the dream interpretation process. I would like to thank David Powell and his team at Freedom Publishing Limited for their fantastic expertise and knowledge and helping to make it such a joy to publish this book.

I have been inspired by so many amazing people that God has brought into my life. I would like to take this opportunity to express my gratitude for the friendship and mentorship of 'Ambassador' Joy Ogwu (former Foreign minister of Nigeria and former President of the United Nations Security Council) who completely embodies the wisdom of God.

A picture paints a thousand words and so I want to thank Julia Powell (Just Believe Prophetic Art) for the inspiring prophetic artwork which brings this book visually alive. Finally, I want to thank the best ever team of three, namely the Trinity of God, the Father, the Son and the Holy Spirit.

Overflowing glory

Preface

On average, people spend 33% of their lives sleeping. Even when our body is asleep, our spirit is still awake. Our dreams are bridges that connect us with the supernatural realm and so Heaven continues to communicate to us as we sleep through our dreams. Dreams access and unlock divine creativity that is deep within us. It is not surprising therefore, that people in history have attributed many inventions and creativity to dreams. For example, the sewing machine, the periodic table, and many artists and writers including the likes of Beethoven, Salvador Dali, Charlotte Brontë, Mary Shelley and Sir Paul McCartney (his "Yesterday" song) credit dreams with some of their most famous creations. Even one of the most powerful, wealthiest and wisest kings in history, namely King Solomon, asked for his wisdom in a dream.

My previous book (*Speakers of Life: How to live a daily prophetic lifestyle*, River Publishing, 2014) touched briefly on the meaning of dreams in a single short chapter. For the last seven years, many people, with and without faith, in many nations have encouraged me to write an entire book dedicated to this topic both on a natural and supernatural level. This is informed by years of experience I have acquired through running dream interpretation workshops, training teams and interpreting dreams in many different settings including pubs, live social media, churches, public buildings, fayres etc.

A significant part of my original inspiration unsurprisingly came from the life and teaching of John Paul Jackson. In the evolution of this book, special mention should go to Natasha Tyrwhitt-Drake who has partnered with me and the rest of the Speakers of Life dream team (in particular Leah, Sue, Lisa 'amigo' and Tim). In addition to her highly tuned dream interpretation gift, one of Natasha's many amazing abilities is to discern and ask the right Heavenly questions to unlock the buried treasures in people. Aspects of this book have directly benefited from her gifts and several examples of dream interpretation in the "Your turn to interpret a dream" chapters (Chapters 3 and 4) have been the result of Natasha and I working together.

This book introduces the principles, process, and application of biblical dream interpretation in both faith-based and secular arenas. It explores the two key components of dream interpretation namely:

1. 'skill is acquired'
2. 'revelation is given'.

On the level of component (1), I use my scientific training to provide a very practical 'How to' guide, which provides plenty of opportunity for the reader to acquire the interpretative skill. On the level of component (2), the book explores the divine love story behind the important 'revelation is given' spiritual component of interpretation.

The book shows how a dream can change a nation by connecting with the author of Heaven's love song, our Heavenly blueprint and our purpose and destiny. As we align to the blueprint of Heaven communicated in our dreams, then we learn to align with the purposes and overtures of Heaven's love song. This causes us to become the right spiritual shape, so that we fit our sphere of influence and then see how a dream can change our community, our land, our nation. My hope and prayer is that this book will be a springboard for you and not a ceiling; and that you will either discover for the first time or fall more deeply in love with the author of Heaven's love song over you.

Chapter 1

THE MOST COMMON DREAM CATEGORIES
Part 1

- Help, My Teeth Are Falling Out!
- Birthing
- Back to School
- Parts of Buildings
- Parts of the Body and Clothing
- Trains, Planes and Automobiles
- I'm Being Chased!

We all dream, irrespective of whether we can remember the dream. Many dreams fall into common categories and categorising the dream helps with the interpreting process. It should be remembered that dreams often overlap in categories. Here are seven of the most common categories; the other ten common categories are addressed in Chapter 5. I have deliberately not put all the common categories into one long chapter, as I have this feeling that after having read about a few categories you'll want to dive straight into the interpretation process which I cover in the next chapter.

Help, My Teeth Are Falling Out!

One day I was talking to a landlord of an English pub as I was wanting to use his upper room to teach dream interpretation classes to teams from our local churches. He was a little uncertain whether it would be a good idea as he was not familiar with dream interpretation. I needed a connection to show it was genuine and that it was helpful to people's lives. I immediately thought of a historical character, the prophet Daniel in the Bible, who supernaturally was given by God the ability or gift to know a person's dream and then interpret it (Daniel 2). Therefore, in the middle of the pub I silently asked the same God in the Bible for the same supernatural gift. Immediately I received the impression or revelation that the pub landlord was having a recurrent dream all about losing his teeth and in addition he was finding difficulty in keeping a grip on some important issues in his life. Equipped with a smile and a handful of boldness and humour I told the landlord about my impressions. To my relief, he was immediately surprised and delighted. Yes indeed, he was having a recurrent dream about losing his teeth.

After some years with his partner they had decided to get married but as the wedding day was approaching, he was finding himself losing a grip on making important decisions as well as running the pub at the same time. As I have learnt from the Bible to see the spiritual reality and revelation of Heaven to be manifest in the physical realm on earth, I asked if I could pray for the landlord. I simply asked for the wisdom and peace of God in the Heavenly realm to come to him right there in the middle of the pub. Well, not only did the wisdom and peace immediately come upon the landlord, it even made him look younger. As an international scientist in the area of skin ageing, this observation did not escape me. The landlord welcomed us to use his upper room for the dream classes, moreover he even encouraged his bar staff to write down their dreams on pieces of paper to give to us for interpretation practice.

This story above highlights a common dream category, namely losing your teeth or the deteriorating condition of your teeth such as the enamel is flaking off, wobbly teeth and so on. Often this dream metaphor represents going through a time of your life where you are losing your grip on a situation in terms of thoughts, emotions and decisions and an increasing inability to chew things over in your mind. We know that the function of teeth is to bite, grip and to chew; therefore in dream language teeth relate to wisdom, clarity of thought and ability to make considered decisions that represent a "win-win" for everyone. Loosing teeth in dreams can reflect a decline in one's ability to steward and express these attributes.

In a spiritual context, it can show that we need to chew more on the holy words of wisdom, such as the Bible, to help with our life decisions. Specific teeth such as a loose eye-tooth can reflect the ability for us to operate in a supernatural way, so that we perceive or fore-know situations/facts or circumstances. The Bible would call this a prophetic or seer gifting. In fact, this type of gifting is so important in the Bible that future prophetic statements make up 27% of its content. Therefore, if you are reading this and you have had many déjà vu experiences, or simply know how and when a conversation or situation will end, then continue to read this book. It will help you to understand this God-given "gift" but also to get to know the giver of this gift. It will help you to realise how you fit into the world and how to talk about your experiences in a way that people will engage with rather than draw ridicule.

Birthing

Sometimes these dreams are about actual childbirth but generally they are more likely to reflect the beginning or birth of a new season or seasons of gifting, opportunity, purpose and destiny coming into your life. The number of months of pregnancy at the point of the birthing is also important as it relates to timing such as being premature or overdue. As we know, timing is essential; if premature then that which is birthed may be vulnerable and not properly developed, while conversely being overdue makes the carrier very tired and fatigued and risks the life of that which is being carried. It may also be relevant whether the birth takes place in a hospital or at home and whether it is a natural delivery or a cesarean section or C-section. A C-section is often linked to birthing things that have an increased seer or perceptive element (see the Birthing Dream in Chapter 3). Pay attention if a name is given to the baby as names often characterise the nature of the new season or gifting or opportunity. For example, the name Isaac means 'laughter' or 'He laughs' which often relates to JOY. Finally, the speed of the baby's development is also important as this can reflect the pace at which the new thing grows. For example, if the baby is walking very early it clearly suggests an accelerated maturity of that which is birthed.

Back to School

These dreams are often centred around a school, college, university or an association with training in a specific job. It can also include the taking of an exam or presenting a lecture in front of people and may also be linked with promotion. You might even be repeating a class or exam that you previously took. All of these may represent that you have an opportunity to learn either from past failures or that you are going to learn something which may feel like going backwards in time. The encouraging aspect of this dream is that this is an opportunity to ensure that you are equipped with something that you will need in the future to deal with an oncoming situation. You might find yourself searching for your next class. This is an indication that guidance is needed for the next step or that you have graduated to the next and more advanced class and thereby represents an upgrade. As always look out in any dreams for puns or play on words; this will be covered in Chapter 5.

Parts of Buildings

This can include dreams involving doors, elevators, stairs, windows, floors of buildings including basements and also entire buildings such as homes, office blocks, hotels and so forth.

A corridor leading you from one place to another place represents a process of transition. It might be that a corridor leads to a door or opening. Doors tend to represent that a change is coming; in other words new opportunities to walk into for the future. In addition, it is important to notice the detail along the corridor or along the journey. For example, there may be paintings of inspirational characters or people on the walls thereby reinforcing the point that it is important to value the journey or process as much as reaching the goal. This principle is mentioned in the Bible in the words of wisdom of King Solomon who encourages us to thoroughly search out the deeper meaning of all that God says (Proverbs 25 verse 2, i.e.25:2).

The process of transition can also be reflected in dreams by elevators or stairs usually indicating that you are rising higher (in terms of responsibility, service or privilege) into the next phase or stage of your life. The prophet Jeremiah talks about a higher calling in our lives that God has for us, to give us a hope and future (Jeremiah, 29:11). Many of you reading this book know that we are on this planet for a greater and higher purpose that is often more than we are currently experiencing. Let's transition into this new reality!!!

The number of floors (note whether it is few or many) that you travel in an elevator or stairs can reflect the degree of advancement in your life or opportunities. It is also important to notice in your dream whether there is a number of the floor (3rd, 4th etc...) at which you get off, as this can also reveal something important. I will cover the spiritual significance of numbers in Chapter 9 but as an appetiser let us consider a few examples. The number eight is often linked to new beginnings or birthing new things as this is the number of people in the Bible who came out of Noah's ark following the flood to begin all over again (1 Peter 3:20). The number nine is often linked to fruitfulness or abundance as this is the number of the fruits of the Holy Spirit described in the Bible (Galatians 5:22). As any fruit salad is far better for the variety of fruits, here are the nine types of spiritual fruit found in the Bible passage: love, joy, peace, patience, kindness, goodness, faithfulness, gentleness and self-control.

Windows can represent increased insight, vision or perception of a particular situation. This can be applied in many facets of our lives, ranging from relationship issues to perceiving market and financial trends in business or scientific breakthroughs. For example, in my case as a scientist, the windows can represent an increased divine revelation and insight about a forthcoming scientific breakthrough (for more of this please see Chapter 7). In data terminology terms it is like having a download from the cloud. In spiritual terms, as a result of my Christian faith, it is receiving a download from the storehouse of God's knowledge in Heaven.

If you are in a place in your dream which is surrounded by windows, then it might be saying that for now you need to observe strategically, to see what is coming and not to be distracted by doing "hands-on" activities. Finally, the size of the window in your dream may be important and the condition of the window, for example, is it clean? The latter may indicate that you might have to attend to certain issues in your life, which have resulted in a dullness of clarity or perception.

The type of building in your dreams is important. A house or your very own house represents your own life, or it can represent a spiritual home such as a church or a place where you have a deep sense of belonging. If the building is a childhood home then it indicates that there are things related to your childhood affecting you now (this can be negative or positive) or it could be things that your family is destined to accomplish, fulfil or inherit.

An office building tends to represent work and your function during the day; therefore, a new office in the building may represent a new role; and if the office is on a higher floor then that suggests promotion. A high-rise building may represent elevated status or level of potential fruitfulness or success in your life. The position where you are situated in the high-rise building may reflect where you are at in this journey.

Rooms of the house also have significance. For example, the attic usually represents either the past, or gifts or memories that you will have received and collected over your life but have not been used or accessed for a long time. If the item in the attic is a family heirloom it could also represent an inheritance that is upon your family (previous generations) which is ready for you to be walking in. If there happens to be dust on these items this usually represents that you have not accessed them for a while signifying a lack of attention, or activity and negligence to these items, lessons learned and memories. The activation of this dream would be to blow off the dust from a gift or ability that you have always had in your life (house) and apply it in a pioneering venture in your life.

A basement in your dream may represent the fact that something is happening which is hidden; it is below the surface and is currently undetected. It can also be something which is happening to your very foundations (often seen in basements) of your life or role (house). The interpretation of this depends upon the context of the dream (see the next chapter) and what the person is doing with the foundations, for example:

a) If the person is destroying the foundations, this represents someone trying to undermine your work-life (office) or home life or spiritual life (your house) or;
b) It might that the person in the dream is killing vermin or termites which might naturally erode the foundations. In this case it represents the good activity of a friend or colleague who is supporting your work, ministry, family in an unseen (basement) selfless way.

Bedrooms can represent a time of rest and restoration, or intimacy or a deep knowing of someone. Bathrooms represent washing off or cleansing certain thought patterns or being affected by certain scenarios at work etc. which have left you feeling "dirty" or grimy" emotionally, psychologically or spiritually. This type of dream overlaps into the cleansing category such as showers or going to the toilet; this is covered in part 2 of the common dream categories (Chapter 5). The living room not surprisingly represents family, community, or connection and this dream might activate a desire to connect with people from whom you have drifted away.

Parts of the Body and Clothing

Clothing tends to represent the putting on of roles that you are designed to do in your daily life. Necklaces, earrings and similar fashion or beauty accessories can represent gifts from well-meaning people or spiritually it can represent gifts from God. The latter are the best type of gifts as they do not come with any strings attached (manipulation), fine print or disclaimers, they are free and always do us good. Shoes can be our journey or walk in life and can have an extra spiritual component of walking in peace (Ephesians 6:15). Depending upon the context of the dream, bare feet can reflect either sensitivity or vulnerability to others and the environment (including pain) or it can simply represent humility and bringing spiritual and experiential peace. The neck can represent being able to turn and see from different angles (enhanced vision, which is good) or conversely if the neck is stiff then it can represent resistance to change or guidance as well as stubbornness. In the Bible, people were referred to as stiff-necked if they did not follow the amazing paths that God had gone to the trouble of preparing for them.

Glasses or spectacles of course represent perception and vision that can also lead to seeing purpose in others and yourself. Ribbons represent reminders of an event, encounter, visit etc… particularly in the context of something that has been planned, agreed or promised. A coat may represent a covering that may protect you and keep you dry and warm which in itself may reflect a degree of insulation against the outside world or circumstances that are around you as you go outside your house (see above for definition of houses). Any clothing that has a particular cultural element or has the colours of a nation or flag may tell you what nation your dream relates to either in the past or future. If it is the future, then it may form part of a deep desire or "calling" to be in that nation or do something with that community of people who may live in your city. An appendage such as an arm or leg which is not functioning normally may mean something emotionally, physically or spiritually that is not fully working yet or undeveloped. A heart may represent many things, such as passion for a cause, direction or principle or sensitivity to the natural or spiritual (a heart of flesh rather than a heart of stone as the Bible calls it in Ezekiel 36:26).

Then there are dreams where you are naked, when you have no clothing. These can represent a cleansing process or freeing from an abundance of unhelpful motives or ideas that have been impressed upon you (like clothes) or a freedom from unhelpful thoughts that would clutter your mind. They can also reflect a greater transparency in your life both to yourself and others and on a spiritual level can represent a move or call to a greater intimacy with God. However, they may simply have no other significance than contain the normal biological and related physical desires that affect most people in a naturally functioning body dream.

Trains, Planes and Automobiles

Transportation features very frequently in dreams. Vehicles often represent or are related to our purpose and reason why we are on the planet. In spiritual terms, transportation may represent the calling of God on our lives for a purpose greater than we perceive ourselves. The size of the vehicle reflects the degree or size of the sphere of the purpose, calling, cause or ministry (please see Chapter 9 for a full list). For example, a car represents a larger influence than a bike and it is likely to involve others as a car will carry passengers.

If we go larger, then buses often represent more passengers or a community associated with your purpose or vision. They may represent a certain maturity or advancement in your purpose or vision; spiritually this may represent a church. Planes can represent organisations and a plane in flight represents something that has really taken off. This may be important if the plane represents an organisation to help people, for example a charity or a business to transform and benefit a city or region. Transport under the ground such as the tube/metro or submarines are groups of people whose role and involvement are more hidden and covert and who may not be interested in public thanks or credit. Anything blown by the wind such as a windsurfer, sailboat or glider represents something that is free to be blown and respond to the wind of opportunity or on a spiritual level, to be blown by the Holy Spirit (John 3:8). If the roof of the vehicle is open or missing it may represent a particular purpose or vision that has "blue sky" thinking, or spiritually it may represent an open-Heaven time with God.

I'm Being Chased

If this is happening in your dream, the interpretation depends on who is chasing you. In other words, does it bring a feeling of fear and panic or does it bring a sense of excitement and purpose? Feeling fear and panic is suggestive of someone or an entity trying to pursue, chase and shut down your purpose or your life – which is clearly bad for you. However, on the other hand, an emotion of excitement, peace and purpose in your dream can represent the passionate pursuit of goodness and blessings in your life. In spiritual terms, the Bible talks about the blessings of God catching us or overtaking us to propel us forward in life at a quicker rate than we could achieve under our own steam (Deuteronomy 28:2). This is clearly good for us and others.

Depending on the context of the dream, the act of being chased in a dream can represent past relationships. The emotion of the dream such as panic, fear, peace or security will tell you if the person or relationship had a good or bad influence in your life. A bad influence may represent you being tempted to go back to old unhealthy patterns of living that you have left behind. A good influence may represent the renewal of good and healthy patterns of living, and the restoring of good things or times that you thought had passed. In this context, the Bible talks about the goodness of God finding us and being so abundant that it restores the years which you thought had been lost and consumed. The Bible uses the metaphor of restoring the years that the locusts had eaten (Joel 2:25).

As you can see with all dreams, it not only depends on the context of the dream but also the source of the dream and we will dive into this and how to interpret a dream more fully in the forthcoming chapters with plenty of opportunity to activate what you have read at the end of many chapters.

So, let's GO DREAM!

Eden

Chapter 2

HOW TO INTERPRET A DREAM IN SIMPLE STEPS

- Simplify the Dream
- Where Are You in the Dream (focus)?
- Context (sub-focus and details)
  - Emotions
  - Night or Day, Colour or Black and White?
  - Time and Numbers
  - Personal Experience
  - Literal Context or Play on Words
- Spiritual Help is Vital in the Interpretation Process

The key strategies for dream interpretation are based around the following three strategies.

1. Simplify the Dream

This follows the "keep it simple" principle. Begin by trying to simplify whatever you can remember of the dream to a few (maximum of three is ideal) key points. This allows us to strip everything back to the basic components and then use this as the foundation to build upon. If you get bogged down in examining every minute detail, your interpretation will likely be too long, unfocussed and confusing. When you are doing this, be mindful of any repeated themes within the single dream or whether the whole dream is a kind of repeat of previous dreams which would constitute a recurring pattern.

For example, are you always being chased (although it maybe by different people), are you always turning up late for events, appointments or meetings (although the details may change), always failing an exam (although the exam subject may be different). Another example, in the Bible, Joseph had two dreams which were part of the same recurring pattern, but the exact details were very different, featuring different symbols. One symbol encompassed sheaves of wheat while the second symbol covered the sun, moon and stars. Both types of symbols were bowing down to Joseph. Despite the different symbols both dreams had the same meaning and were therefore part of a dream pattern. The meaning was speaking to Joseph's destiny and future where his family did actually bow down to Joseph because of his royal promotion in Pharaoh's court in Egypt.

As you are reading this, is there an area of your life that your recurring dream is speaking about which could be pointing to your destiny and purpose on planet earth?

2. Where Are You in the Dream (focus)?

This question relates to the focus of the dream and the answer can be summarised to three possibilities.

A) Are you the focus in the dream? In other words, are people watching you or if you were not in the dream, would the whole dream fall apart? If the answer is yes, then the dream is directly about you. Then the next thing is to identify where you are and what you are doing, and this may reflect your daily role, activity or occupation. For example, in the Bible there are a couple of well-known dreams featuring two occupations, namely a baker and a cupbearer to the King (Genesis 40), but with contrasting outcomes.

B) Are you observing in the dream? If this true, then the dream is not primarily about you but you may have a role as a witness, or an encourager from afar. In the spiritual context, this may take the form of someone who petitions or intercedes, cries out on behalf of others or brings a scenario to the attention of God for the opportunity of intervention. Is the central character of the dream male or female, young or old and do you know them? Are they a leader or influencer? Is there a strange or familiar feel about the person? In other words, is there a sense of peace and wellbeing or familiarity which is likely to indicate a sense of encouragement and a place of safety for the source of the dream (see Chapter 7)?

However, in quite a number of cases there might be a faceless person, or someone where you never get a good view of their face, and who has a sense of peace and encouragement and maybe even offers help in the dream. If this happens in a dream it is a strong indicator in the spiritual realm that the person is an angel or the Holy Spirit as described in the Bible. If the person you are observing is a stranger with an uneasy feel then most likely the dream is some sort of warning or danger.

C) Are you participating in the dream? In other words, while you are not the main focus of the dream, are you are interacting, for example by encouraging, safeguarding, cheering on, keeping a helpful eye on things? All of this may indicate that you may have a role where you are meant to help others in a particular way that would benefit everyone and make use of your resources and gifts and talents.

3. Context (sub-focus and details)

Context is very important and it is also vital to identify the sub-focus elements of the dream as well as details that help us to tease out the key factors from what might be lots of peripheral detail that is not related to the core of the dream. The scientist would call this process, the detection of the signal from the background noise. Therefore, it is always good to start with a few questions that will help in this process. These are:

- What were the strong emotions in the dream?
- Was it night or day in your dream?
- Was the dream in colour (and if so which colours) or black and white?
- Do you remember the time you had the dream and were there any important time/s or numbers in the dream?
- Was there any personal experience and literal context?

Let's consider each of these in turn:

Emotions. The stronger the emotion, the greater importance it has in the dream. This helps us to clarify the dream and remove any peripheral emotions. In addition, if a strong emotion is linked with an object or person then it helps us to identify the key sub-focus and detail elements in the dream. These emotions can include a positive or negative feeling, but in addition, did the strong emotion bring a sense of love or fear, security or danger? This helps not only to determine the source of the dream but whether the dream is a warning or an encouragement, either to help you in your destiny or to help others in their destiny.

Night or Day; Colour or Black and White. If a dream is either at night and/or in black and white and full of fear, then this often suggests that the source of the dream is intended for harm or to have evil intent such as intimidation or the dream may represent a warning. In contrast, a dream in colour, during the day and with emotions of peace, wellbeing, freedom and safety suggests that the dream is speaking to and calling out your destiny and in a biblical and spiritual context of interpretation this dream is likely to be from God. If the dream is in colour, then the type of colour can be important. The significance of colours, numbers and other symbols in a dream will be dealt in greater detail in Chapter 9.

However, as a sneak preview, it is worth highlighting here the importance of context. For example, the colour red can mean royalty, power, war, anger, bloodshed, or sacrifice. If there is a dream where someone gives their life to save someone else, then the colour red has to do with sacrifice and possibly atonement; it is definitely not to do with anger or war in this context. Therefore, I cannot emphasise enough that dream interpretation should NOT be carried out in a computational type of way simply using check lists of what things mean. It depends very strongly on the context in which the objects, colours, etc. are found. In addition, many of these derivations and references have a spiritual connotation and link all the way back to the Bible (see Isaiah 1:18, Revelation, 6:4; 12:3; 2 Kings 3:22, Joshua 2:18-21 for the colour red) which is why biblical dream interpretation is so helpful as it often releases aspects of your life destiny.

The intensity or brightness of the colour can also be important. For example, the colour green often symbolises fruitfulness in dreams. A pastel colour of green could denote that the fruitfulness is starting from a place where it has enormous potential to grow stronger, which is usually represented by a brighter green. Conversely, a pastel shade may also represent a fading from what it was, and this depends again on the context. As a general rule, if you can remember clearly certain aspects of the dream but cannot remember any colours/numbers etc. then it is likely that they are not important and so move on. This is particularly important when you are reducing the dream to its constituent parts as detailed in section 1) above.

Time and Numbers. The aspect of time has two contexts. The first is the noting of any times in the actual dream. Secondly and equally important, it is important to note the time or times you may actually wake up whilst having the dream as well as at the end of the dream. Time consists of an arrangement of numbers and the Bible is enormously helpful to explain what these numbers often mean, simply because they have spiritual significance in the Bible. This detailed aspect of numbers is addressed in Chapter 9. As a small example, if you wake up at 3.33 it is a strong indicator that God could be giving you wisdom, invention, innovation and ideas that are beyond that which you can generate yourself, in other words divine revelation. This is because the book of the prophet Jeremiah 33:3 says:

Call to me and I will answer you and tell you great and unsearchable things you do not know.

It is also important to note any numbers that you see in a dream. For example, I often have dreams featuring numbers which relate to the actual birthday or anniversaries of people I will meet in the future. The numbers themselves have a meaning which helps to encourage and unlock the potential of that person or couple.

Personal Experience. Another example of context is what the symbol means to the dreamer in terms of their own personal experience. For example, a dream featuring a dog or a pack of dogs may have a completely different meaning depending upon whether the dreamer has a love or a fear of dogs, according to their own personal experience. There is another layer on top of this, as certain animals or objects may have a particular spiritual, elevated, or inferior context within a societal culture or faith system; again depending upon the individual who had the dream. The Bible provides many great examples of context. One example involves Gideon who was raised up by God to help rescue Israel from oppression as recorded in Judges 7:9-15. Gideon needed some encouragement on the night before the crucial battle, particularly as he was severely outnumbered by the Midianites and Amalekites. He crept into the enemy camp with his servant and overheard one of the Midianites relating a dream to his friend about a barley bread loaf rolling into the camp and causing great destruction. At that point, Gideon knew that victory was guaranteed; he knew the barley bread was himself and his army as he had been raised as a thresher of barley and wheat to make bread.

Literal Context or Play on Words. Sometimes the symbol has a direct literal meaning, for example if a Christian saw a mustard seed in a dream, then it might simply mean a representation of the Kingdom of God because it literally says in the Bible that the Kingdom of God is like a mustard seed (Mark 4:30-31). Sometimes there is a play on words with either the actual name of the dreamer (if the dream is about them as the main focus) or within the dream story itself.

For example, in 2016, I was interpreting a dream for a colleague of a good friend of mine. In addition to the actual content of the dream, I felt a spiritual prompting that the name of the dreamer was significant. Without going into the details of the dream it centred upon the fact that we are all the very aspect of joy in the eye of Jesus (we are the joy set before him as he endured the crucifixion on the cross, Hebrews 12:2). Interestingly the name of the dreamer contained the letters "Trist" and the context of the dream was all about exchanging sadness for joy; a picture of a divine exchange. Well, for those who speak French the work for sadness is "triste" which is very close to part of the name of the dreamer. Therefore, the powerful interpretation revealed that the sadness which had followed the dreamer for most of their life (even their name meant sadness) was about to be broken off and then exchanged for joy. This is indeed what happened as the dreamer invited Jesus into their life, a beautiful moment!

Spiritual Help is Vital in the Interpretation Process

The knowledge of the symbolism and the context of these dream symbols as described above represents the skill component of dream interpretation. However, there is another layer, which is the spiritual component of dream interpretation; this is the revelation part as it is revealed to us from outside of ourselves. This is a major distinguishing factor from the Freud and Jung models of dream interpretation as they primarily ignore this spiritual component to instead focus on the self and human psyche, i.e. within ourselves. Within the context of spiritual revelation, it is clearly important to identify the nature of the spiritual source of help as there are many faiths, belief systems and spiritual beings.

Angels. In the Bible we find that not only do all "(dream) interpretations belong to God" (Genesis 40:8, Daniel 2:28) but that there are specific angels dispatched by God to help us not only in certain facets of dream interpretation but their name actually gives us a clue as to their role. For example, let's take the examples of two angels, Palmoni and Gabriel who helped Daniel in the Bible. Daniel interpreted many dreams for the courts of the King of Babylon who had taken Daniel's own people into slavery. In Daniel 8:13 following a dream that Daniel did not understand we read:

> *Then I heard one saint speaking, and another saint said unto* ***that certain saint*** *which spake, How long shall be the vision... (NKJV emphasis added).*

The Bible scholars identify "that certain saint" as an angel with the Hebrew name of 'PALMONI'. In this scripture, Palmoni is helping Daniel to understand the number of years for the realisation of the dream. What is amazing is that the actual meaning of the Hebrew name Palmoni is 'the numberer of secrets", or "the wonderful numberer". Therefore, here we see that one angelic function is to do with the numbers of God. More details on this can be found in the writings of two 19th century writers, Francis John Bodfield Hooper and Milo Mahan who wrote entire books on this subject (see Chapter 10 for details). In Chapters 3 and 4, I have included some examples of the meaning of numbers in dreams. I am so glad we have angelic help in this interpretation process.

Another example of angelic help comes in the form of the archangel Gabriel who said to Daniel "*I have now come to give you insight and understanding*" (Daniel 9:22). Gabriel's role here is to help Daniel in dream interpretation but he has other roles as a herald to the birth of John the Baptist (Luke 1:19) and Jesus when he spoke to Zechariah and Mary respectively (Luke 1:19 and 26).

The God of Heaven. The Bible says that all "*interpretations belong to God*" (Genesis 40:8) and so it makes sense to ask him for those interpretations. As a Christian, I clearly believe that God's love for me every second of every day calls out my destiny which is more amazing that I can ever think of or imagine (Ephesians 3:20) by myself. Furthermore, no other God has ever given his son (Jesus) to die for me. Therefore, the spiritual component for me is both the written word of God in the Bible but also the living word of God which is revealed by the Holy Spirit. The two components of biblical dream interpretation can be summarised by the phrase: **skill is acquired; revelation is given**. The love of God is the revelation component, it is given to us by a benevolent, ever loving God who sings over us even at night when our heart is awake even though we are asleep (Song of Songs 5:2). This spiritual reality is covered later by the Divine Love Story (Chapters 7 & 8 respectively). However suffice it to say at this point that the depth and clarity of the revelation/spiritual component of dream interpretation is sharpened and enhanced by a greater intimacy with the love of God.

Let's go spiritually deeper and ask the following question. If all interpretations belong to God and we can receive revelation from God then does it figure that God can reveal to us not only the very dreams that people have before they can tell it to us, but in addition God can give us the interpretation as well in advance? That sounds the sort of thing we only witness on the movie screen like the Marvel superheroes and X-men who can read minds. Well the answer to the previous question is yes. This is why the revelation component is so key in the process of dream interpretation. The very first recorded happening of this is not in a movie blockbuster or a science fiction book but actually in the Bible.

There is the account of Daniel who was taken into exile, from Jerusalem to Babylon, by King Nebuchadnezzar and was known amongst other things for his amazing dream interpreting skills as a result of his faith in God. In one example, God allowed Daniel to know King Nebuchadnezzar's dream without the king telling it to anyone, but God also then gave Daniel the interpretation for the king. Back in January 2014 I was reading this account in the Bible (Daniel 2) and I said to God, 'today is my birthday I would love to have this "Daniel" gift as my birthday present so that I can help others'. Well, within a few hours I had the opportunity to step into and exercise this gift to the amazement of myself and the dreamer. Not only did I recount their whole dream but also gave them the interpretation before they even had a chance to tell me the dream. The dreamer had previously tried for several years telling people their dream and seeking for an interpretation but was without any success.

Gifts, like the one God gave to me, tend to grow with use and exercise very much like any muscle in our body. Therefore since 2014, I have exercised this gift and asked God's spirit to train me. As a result, I have used this gift many times and in many countries across the world with people from different walks of life and a significant number of those have not had any spiritual grid for their lives. In all cases the result has been positively life changing for everyone concerned.

Another example was during an event that our community interest company (Speakers of Life) was co-hosting with a local Anglican Church at a pub in Prudhoe, a small town in the rural part of the north east of England. As I was leaning against the bar waiting for the server to finish serving others, God told me the recurrent dream that she had been having and what it meant. At a suitable moment (I didn't want her to be unduly surprised and drop the beer glasses) I relayed this revelation to her, and she was very surprised and delighted as it had been troubling her. My friend and I felt this was linked somehow to some back pain, which God also told us about, that she had been suffering with for some considerable time. As a result, she waited for a five minute gap where she did not have to work at the bar, then came across to us; we prayed a simple prayer and God healed her back completely. It was a great evening for her, a 100% healed back, insight into her dream and what she could do about it. She then wanted to know more about the God who had done all of this for her.

In summary, the points above provide a symbolic and contextual understanding but it is important to realise that the key to understanding dreams uses a combination of symbolic understanding plus the ability to hear God's voice (i.e. skill is acquired and revelation is given). The written or logos word of God in the Bible is full of parables and allegories which can help us alongside the word of God in our hearts (or rhema word) by his Holy Spirit. Even with all the tools and categories of dream symbols described above and in later chapters, it is vitally important to understand that we still need to rely on the Holy Spirit for the revelation and definitely not on other methods using Freud, Jung or indeed Google (which will draw from an unequal and potentially confusing combination of Jung, Freud, Bible, and New Age spirituality to name a few).

Open heaven

Chapter 3

YOUR TURN TO INTERPRET A DREAM
Part 1 – Simple Dreams

Systematic activation of Chapter 2 teaching

- Dream 1: Birthing
- Dream 2: Let's Bake some Bread
- Dream 3: Five Cows
- Dream 4: Up the Mountain
- Dream 5: Fill the Empty Seats

Now before you read any further, I would like to encourage you to have a go and use the principles and skills described above to write down what you think is the interpretation of the dreams that are detailed below. To make it even more fun why not do it with a friend on social media, in a café or at home and then compare notes. This provides a safe environment where we can give permission to each other to get it wrong and make mistakes but importantly to celebrate that we have tried and that this is the real success. Remember, if you get bogged down in examining every minute detail then your interpretation will likely be too long, unfocussed and confusing.

These exercises will help to train and tune your dream interpretation skill levels. In the context of the two interpretation components, **skill is acquired, and revelation is given**, it is also ok to ask for spiritual help. As an illustration, there is a world-wide TV quiz game called "Who wants to be a Millionaire" and one of the available help options for the struggling contestant is to phone a friend who is hopefully the expert with the answer. This is a one-time option in the game show. Well the Bible tells us that the God of Heaven has the revelation for all the dream interpretations, which automatically makes Him the expert without equal. In addition, you can ask Him all of the time through prayer, it is not just the one-off phone a friend option. We are all spiritually hardwired to connect with the God of Heaven, and we have access through Jesus. Sounds like a great deal I know; we can ask for unlimited help and it will not cost us anything as the price has already been paid by Jesus (which is a deep and profound treasure).

If this sounds like a great option but you don't know how to begin or progress then please jump to the chapters later in the book entitled 'The Divine Love Story parts 1 and 2' (Chapters 7 and 8). These enable you both to start and go deeper, or if this is your very first time wanting to connect with your spiritual help though Jesus, then there is a simple prayer on the first page of Chapter 10 which will help you.

Great, I know we are all at different stages of the journey, but I think it is time to try these activation exercises. You can always take a break if you are struggling and maybe "phone" our spiritual help, the God of Heaven, have a go and have fun!!

Dream 1: Birthing

This dream was received from the UK in 2020, during the writing of this book.

> *I dreamt that I was pregnant. I was full term and ready to give birth. I was in this room that sort of looked like a classroom and everyone was panicking around me because there was nowhere for me to give birth. Everyone was rushing around because no one knew what was happening or could find room for me to give birth. I was then taken to hospital and I began to give birth but I couldn't give natural birth so had to have a C-section. I could see the doctor very clearly giving me the operation and taking out the baby. It was a baby boy and we*

named him Hosea. I just remember looking at the baby with an overwhelming sense of joy and gratitude. And then it ended with little Hosea (who was now walking) standing in a doorway and everyone was just looking at him in awe. I remember his eyes were bright blue.

Here is the interpretation, using the three steps detailed in Chapter 2.

1) **Simplify the Dream.** If we wanted to simplify the dream to three sentences, we would write the following:

- The dreamer was pregnant, she was in a classroom and was ready to give birth.
- In a hospital the dreamer had a C-section and gave birth to a baby boy naming him Hosea.
- The dream ended with the blue-eyed little Hosea standing in a doorway and everyone was just looking at him in awe.

2) **Focus.** The dreamer is the focus of the dream because if you take them out of the dream then the dream itself falls apart.

3) **Context (sub-focus and details):** When we do not know whether it is night or day then we look to see if there is any colour or positive emotion in the dream as opposed to black and white and negative emotion. We see that there is colour (blue eyes) but there are also positives such as giving birth. Even though there are some negative emotions such as panic there are stronger and more numerous positive emotions in the dream. For example, there was an "overwhelming sense of joy and gratitude" and people looked at Hosea with a sense of awe. Therefore, before we look for the sub-focus, we see from the details that this dream is positive. There are no elements of time or particular personal experience mentioned by the dreamer. This means we can go on to the sub-focus in detail. There are five main points of sub-focus in this dream and these are (in the order that they occur in the dream):

Pregnant, Classroom, C-section, Hosea, Doorway

Let's take these in order. The dreamer is **pregnant** with something new, a gift! Being pregnant or giving birth is one of the top common dreams as we have already covered in the previous chapter. When asking questions of the dreamer, she personally told us that she has never been pregnant with a physical baby and so here the pregnancy is clearly a metaphor for her signifying the imminent birth of something new in her life. Let's take a pause here to emphasise the fact that it is ok and necessary at times to question the dreamer for clarification once they have told you their dream. Ask the questions about emotions, colour etc. as they may not have remembered until you ask them. This is part of the 'skill is acquired' component of dream interpretation that we can learn, namely interviewing the dreamer.

Ok, going back to the dream interpretation, the initial place of the dream is in a **classroom**. Classrooms, schools, college, universities in dreams all represent a place or season of learning and growth. Do not see it as a regressing back to school but see it as being given an opportunity to learn something which you may have missed out on or forgotten. This new opportunity to learn is going to be extremely useful for your next stage in life and walking out your destiny.

What the dreamer is carrying might concern others because they are not sure either (1) where this will fit or how to deliver and carry this new thing or gift appropriately or (2) how is it going to be birthed in a classroom. The dreamer does not have to be worried about this because the baby is born in a hospital by **C-section**.

The phrase C-section often has a doubled meaning. The first can be literal i.e. a caesarean section, namely a surgical procedure used to deliver a baby through incisions in the abdomen and uterus. Second, in dream language it often speaks of spiritual seer gifting, a play on words with the letter C and the word "see". In the Bible a seer is prophetically gifted to "see" things in the Spirit realm, such as details of an event before it happens or things about a person before they have ever met them, such as their name, appearance and so on. The

C-section reference in the dream clearly speaks about a seer gifting being birthed and perhaps the child being called to a lifestyle of being a seer as part of their prophetic destiny.

This fits with the name given to the baby, which was **Hosea** who was a prophet in the Bible. The name Hosea actually means 'salvation'. Therefore, this gives a clue to the purpose of this new seer gifting for the dreamer which is to bring salvation. This can be applied in several ways ranging from scenarios such as saving or rescuing situations or people which are heading towards a bad outcome, or to scenarios where there would be a spiritual rescuing of the direction of people's lives. In biblical terms this would typically be expressed as the rescuing or salvation of people's souls by giving their lives to Jesus. Put it this way, if we view driving a car as a metaphor for having control of our life and destiny then giving your life to Jesus is about handing over the driving of your car or life to a much better driver, who knows where they are going and the destination is so much better.

The final part of the dream shows that this seer gifting will grow quickly. This is represented in the dream by the fact that baby Hosea had already matured to a walking stage. Importantly, this seer gifting would open opportunities, which is represented by Hosea standing in a **doorway**. Doorways in dreams always tend to represent opportunities to walk from one situation, realm or scenario into another one. This could also represent a transition from the old to the new or from a place which is "restricted" or closed to a place of freedom which feels like a spacious place. The door may represent the entire transitional stage or simply a stepping stone in this process. The bright blue eyes of Hosea speak about the spiritual or supernatural aspect of the seer gifting. In biblical dream interpretation, blue usually represents Heaven and communion with God (see meaning of colours in Chapter 9). Therefore, the dreamer will perceive the things of Heaven, either for the first time or as an upgrade to their existing gifting. This awareness or revelation of Heaven or Heavenly encounters will increase as the dreamer's communion with the God of Heaven increases.

Dream 2: Let's Bake some Bread

This dream was sent in 2017 from a UK dreamer.

> *I held a loaf of bread (like a crusty French loaf) in my hands. I think I was about to put it into the oven to bake. But I was wondering if it would be ready before my youngest daughter brought me a loaf. She and I were baking for each other as a regular occurrence, we were anxiously waiting to see whose bread would be ready first (not in a fun, playful kind of way; but a serious task). Also, as I woke I 'remembered' that I'd had this dream for the previous two nights.*

Here is the interpretation using the three steps detailed in the previous chapter.

1) **Simplify the Dream**. If we wanted to simplify the dream to a maximum of three sentences, we would write the following, in fact it can be summarised in two sentences:

- The dreamer was baking bread with her youngest daughter as a regular occurrence.
- They were anxiously waiting to see whose bread would be ready first.

2) **Focus**. The dreamer is the focus of the dream because if you take them out of the dream then the dream falls apart.

3) **Context (sub-focus and details):** As this is a simple dream there are only three main points of sub-focus and these are (in the order that they occur in the dream):

Dreamer, Bread, Daughter

In terms of a superficial interpretation, the dream is very much about the relationship between the **dreamer** (mother) and her youngest

daughter. The **bread** is symbolic of what the mother has put into the life of her daughter. The baking of the bread is like the process of waiting to see what the fruit of that will be. That is why it is serious and not fun because the mother is tempted to also bake the same bread just in case her daughter's bread does not turn out right, as expected or on time. The mother appears concerned or worried about whether she has put enough into her daughter (e.g. wisdom, truth, knowledge, guidance, time) and the anxiety around that is felt by both of them, when waiting to see which loaf is ready. It also reflects that baking is a process that takes time and cannot be hurried, which also speaks to the development of the things that the mother has passed on to the daughter.

The fact that the dream was repeated suggests that it is important for that time and there might also be a second deeper level to the dream. Therefore, if we dig a little deeper, we see in the dream that the bread represents provision. Given that the daughter is also baking her own bread too, it is a case of her exploring and figuring out what provision or life skills she has received and what she can choose to do with them. The dream suggests that it is the eve of a season change where the mother would be free to help the daughter explore and steward what she has been given and not be anxious about it being different, unusual or something unexpected.

In addition, as the dreamer was a woman of Christian faith it points to the fact that there should be no anxiety about the continued provision from God either to the mother and then passing this on the daughter or directly to the daughter (i.e. her own bread). This principle is found in 2 Corinthians 9:10-11:

> *Now he who supplies seed to the sower and bread for food will also supply and increase your store of seed and will enlarge the harvest of your righteousness. You will be made rich in every way so that you can be generous on every occasion, and through us your generosity will result in thanksgiving to God.*

Dream 3: Five Cows

This was a dream that sent to me from the UK in the summer of 2019.

> *I was on a large pitch like a football pitch. There were spectators on a tiered seating area watching the pitch. On this pitch there were 5 cows. 2 of them had riders and were leaving the pitch. The 3 remaining cows were in the middle of the field. They were fat. Two of them were red and I was sat on the third one. I don't know what colour that one was. The cows were all kneeling down with their bottoms in the air, like elephants do when they are in a circus ring. Suddenly I heard a shrill whistle like a referee's whistle. I said to myself 'here we go' and shifted my seating on the cow so that I wouldn't fall off when it stood up as I thought the whistle would mean it was now time for these 3 cows to move... but none of them moved. I said to the cow 'hey what's happening', he spoke to me with his eyes closed, chewing the cud and said "Oh sometimes they leave us for up to an hour". Then I woke up.*

Here is the interpretation using the three steps detailed in the previous chapter.

1) **Simplify the Dream**. If we wanted to simplify the dream to three sentences, we would write the following:

- The dreamer was on a large pitch with 5 cows surrounded by spectators.
- 2 cows left while 3 fat ones remained kneeling down like elephants in a circus ring.
- Following a shrill whistle, the dreamer expected the cows to move but they didn't and the cow underneath the dreamer explained the reason.

2) **Focus**. The dreamer is the focus of the dream because if you remove them from the dream it falls apart.

3) **Context (sub-focus and details):** The main points of sub-focus in this dream (in the order they appear are):

Spectator-surrounded pitch (stadium)
5 cows (2 departed, 3 remained)
Remaining cows kneeled like circus elephants
The cows did not move to the whistle.

The fact that this is a **spectator-surrounded pitch** implies that most of the people (or the community which the dreamer is part of) are passive; they are not participating. They prefer to watch others provide the action, almost like watching a performance. In the context of this dream, the **cows** were described as fat and therefore represent prosperity and provision, in a similar manner to the meaning of "cash cows" in business slang today. Cows in the Bible were used to tread out the corn, for ploughing, etc. which again represents provision, effort (industry) and resource. This resource could be physical such as workers and finances or spiritual such as God given gifts and strategy. Either way, they were in great abundance as the cows were fat.

There were **5 cows;** the number 5 represents grace (see Chapter 9) and so there is a grace on this season to move forward with the resources that have been given. The fact that it occurred within the parameters of the stadium implies that this season of grace is not only for the dreamer but also for those spectators who would want to participate. The two cows departing the stadium represents abundance and provision leaving the stadium. This is the only "movement" in the dream. The **2 cows** went out together and cows are often yoked in pairs when they are working. The number 2 often symbolises witness, agreement or testimony (see Chapter 9) and so there is agreement with the purpose for which these cows were given, and their sphere of influence was outside the stadium.

This outgoing function contrasts with the inward looking, spectator mode in the stadium. This implies that the stadium could be a church (as the dreamer was a Christian leader) or a community, or a business group. The fact that the two departing cows were being ridden implies that there is a plan and strategy to direct the resource (i.e. the cows).

The dreamer stays on the pitch with the **remaining 3 cows**. The number 3 symbolises divine completeness or resurrection (see Chapter 9). Two of the cows were red which often symbolises power and authority, depending on the context. The dreamer sees that the remaining resources are all that is required to have a powerful natural and spiritual impact (even reviving things that appear dead or finished) when they are put to work. The dreamer was sat on one of the cows which suggests a strategic leadership role as they steward the resources with which they have been entrusted. They are gifted with the ability to steer or direct the resources (cows). The ability of the dreamer to manage the resources is shown by the way the dreamer adjusts their seating position on the cow as they anticipated its movement following the whistle.

However, there is clearly a warning in the dream about resources not working as they should. This misalignment is symbolised in two ways by the posture of the cows, firstly the **kneeling down like circus elephants** and secondly the lazy posture at the end of the dream. Cows do not kneel like circus elephants and so the resources are not behaving as they should. In addition, the circus scenario reiterates the fact that the spectators in the stadium are not participating in the action on the pitch, they are content to watch the performance and be entertained.

This is re-emphasised when we see that **the cows did not move to the whistle** which was an official (referee) sign to get moving. This is a lazy posture. The result is that the resources which the dreamer has been entrusted with to manage and lead (symbolised by being seated on the cow) are not pulling their weight at this time and are simply not doing what they are expected to do (the dreamer's adjustment on the seat in anticipation of this).

The resources themselves do not have the vision (symbolised by the closed eyes of the cow) to see their own timing or purpose and are content to ruminate on things (symbolised by chewing the cud) rather than getting to action. The sluggish and unmoving fat cows symbolise inefficient and inactive wealth and resources. Furthermore, there is no urgency, as shown by the resources being content to wait up to an hour in the dream. This represents the missing of a timely opportunity (the referee's whistle) where the resources need to move and be deployed to where they are needed (i.e. outside of the stadium where the other two cows went). There seems to be a spirit of overly satisfied comfort in this dream where the majority (spectators) are not motivated to do anything about the resources they have been given for the benefit of others (e.g. their community outside the stadium) and are content to watch the few do almost everything.

As the dreamer was a Christian, this scenario could represent a church which is all about entertaining the congregation and the "seated" people are willing to spectate while the process of serving the outside community using the provided resources is either not an urgent priority or there is a blindness to it.

Apart from the wakeup call to the spectators, a possible application of the dream is that the cows need to be trained or "broken in" so they can be directed to where they are needed. There are several Bible verses illustrating this, Jeremiah 31:18, Hosea 4:16 and Hosea 10:11. It is an encouragement to the dreamer to persevere even when people or finances do not do what they are designed to do (e.g. cows kneeling down). It is clear that the dreamer needs a partner to help share the load and responsibility in order to get things moving as the dreamer was the only one person for three cows. Each cow needs a rider as suggested by the two which left the pitch each having a rider.

Dream 4: Up the Mountain

This is a dream that was sent from the USA during April 2020.

I was running down a mountain along a windy foot path. I was barefoot. As soon as I got to the bottom of the mountain, I immediately started running up the next mountain in front of me. I looked down at my feet and noticed that I now had clean white crew socks on. The path was not a dirt surface, I'm running up smooth steps, like prepared marble and a solid surface. I had a sense in the dream that I know where I'm going, like I've been there before. I was climbing, climbing and when I got to the top of the stairs and the mountain, there was a gate. The gate was not a fancy gate, maybe 3 feet x 5 feet wooden gate; a bit like a gate to someone's home, like a path gate or a back yard/side gate. I see a prepared platform that's raised up about 1-2 feet. I also see a pair of men's trousers with the belt still in the loops. They weren't folded. It's like the person who had been wearing them stood up, loosened the belt, dropped them and stepped out of them. I feel like I sat down outside the gate. Next thing I remember is seeing the sky light up, not with fireworks, but illuminated in light. I feel like it was celebrating.

Here is the interpretation using the three steps detailed in the previous chapter.

1) **Simplify the Dream** to three sentences:

- The dreamer runs barefoot down a rough path mountain and then runs up a smooth mountain path wearing white socks.
- At the top of the next mountain there was an ordinary looking gate and a raised platform with a pair of abandoned men's trousers.
- The dream ends with a celebration of the sky lighting up.

2) **Focus**. The dreamer is the focus of the dream because if you take them out of the dream then the dream falls apart.

3) **Context (sub-focus and details):** There are six main points of sub-focus in this dream and these are (in the order that they occur in the dream):

Mountain, Feet, Gate, Platform, Trousers, Sky Lighting up

The dreamer, who we knew was a Christian, has to be on the correct **mountain** of influence for them to find their sphere of influence. This is seen by the following scripture in the Bible where Paul says:

> *We, however, will not boast beyond proper limits, but will confine our boasting to the sphere of service God himself has assigned to us, a sphere that also includes you.* 2 Corinthians 10:13.

Therefore, the dreamer has to leave the mountain they are on and transition to another mountain. Leaving this mountain requires vulnerability (**barefoot**) and may not be straight forward or pleasant, as symbolised by the dirt covered windy path. The encouraging aspect is that the journey becomes much easier once they begin to climb the mountain which they are supposed to be occupying, as it is their mountain or sphere of influence.

In fact, the ascent is made easier not only by the provision of a smooth surface but also by the path becoming a series of steps. The dreamer's **feet** are no longer bare but covered in white socks which speaks of protection, purity, cleansing but also holiness (see Chapter 1). The ascent with these components of holiness, cleansing and purity is mentioned in Psalm 24:3-4:

> *Who may ascend the mountain of the Lord? Who may stand in his holy place? The one who has clean hands and a pure heart.*

Therefore, the dreamer is already equipped to ascend this "holy" hill of influence. What is more they already have access not though their own efforts but by the sacrifice of Jesus on the cross that gave us our clean hands and pure heart through His shed blood. This access is represented by the **gate,** the ease and simplicity of the way made for us by the cross of Christ is shown by the fact that the gate is "not fancy" and that it is made of wood (symbolising the wooden cross). In John 10:7-9 we read:

> *Jesus said again, "Very truly I tell you, I am the gate for the sheep. All who have come before me are thieves and robbers, but the sheep have not listened to them. I am the gate; whoever enters through me will be saved."*

The calling and gifting upon the dreamer is to occupy a **platform** which has been previously occupied by men and the tradition of men (i.e. **men's trousers**) and which has been vacated in a hurried manner (trousers not folded). The dreamer is a little reticent (possibly due to previous gender bias in the Church or denomination) to step into the trousers, hence waiting at the gate.

The outcome of the dreamer stepping on the platform (and wearing the trousers) will result in the **sky lighting up,** in other words the dreamer having a high overarching influence which is very visible and illuminated by the light of Jesus, not by the efforts of man (fireworks). This speaks to Philippians 2:15-16:

> *Then you will shine among them like stars in the sky as you hold firmly to the word of life.*

Dream 5: Fill the Empty Seats

This is a dream that was given to me for interpretation in 2017 by a friend living in the New York area and attending a church on Manhattan Island. This dream was received by the dreamer about 3-4 weeks before I was due to preach at the Manhattan Island church and so the preacher in the dream is me.

> *We were at church for Sunday service and Mark (scientist from the UK) was preaching. He was giving words of knowledge and said "is there someone who does A.V. (Audio/visual) and*

scheduling?" I was sitting on the floor behind a pew (even though our Church does not have pews, it did in the dream for whatever reason) and my husband nudged me and urged "that's you, get up!" Mark pointed to me and said "see all these empty seats, you need to pray them in. And if anyone else wants to stand in intercession get up now and I will invest $0.50 per person." People started rushing up in a line to volunteer. Then I woke up!

Here is the interpretation using the 3 steps detailed in the previous chapter.

1) **Simplify the Dream** to three sentences:

- The Sunday preacher (Mark) in the Church gave words of knowledge and then pointed at the dreamer who was sitting down.
- The dreamer's husband encouraged the dreamer to get up and respond to the preacher's request for intercessors.
- The dream ends with people rushing to volunteer.

2) **Focus**. This is an interesting dream as the main focus is split between two people, the dreamer and the preacher. If you take either of them out of the dream, then the dream falls apart. However, if you have to choose only one then it is always worth noting that the focus of a dream is often a person who is pointed at or highlighted and in this case it is the dreamer.

3) **Context (sub-focus and details, anything unusual)**: There are six main points of sub-focus in this dream and these are (in the order that they occur in the dream):

Preacher, A/V Audio Visual and Scheduling,
Pews, Nudging Husband, Intercession, $0.50

The **preacher** is known by the dreamer and therefore represents a trusted and ordered (symbolised as a scientist) source of encouragement and knowledge as shown by the words of knowledge they give. For those who are not familiar with the Holy Spirit gift of words of knowledge, it can be defined as a revelation of a fact for which there is no prior knowledge, and which concerns the past or present but not the future. In addition, the context was a church, symbolising a safe place for the dreamer, and it was a Sunday thereby signifying a holy day.

The **AV/ Audio Visual** and **scheduling** speaks not only about spiritual hearing (Audio) and spiritual sight (Visual) but also about the timing of these gifts in terms of perception of times and seasons, together with the wisdom of the timing (i.e. **scheduling**).

The **pews** speak to this idea of orderliness. The things which are to come in this dream will be organised and well-timed and they will depend on the dreamer's ability or gift to spiritually see and hear what the Spirit of God is doing. Even though the dreamer is pointed at to get up, there is also a corporate participation and encouragement as shown by the **nudging husband**. This encouragement is necessary because the dreamer has to take their place in the new scenario, to change their position, availability or attitude as shown in the dream by shift from a sitting down position to getting up (i.e. from passive to active).

The specific ministry for the dreamer (and others as shown at the end of the dream) is **intercession,** to bring people into the Church so that they can engage more deeply in their faith or simply so that they can find faith in Jesus. The gathering of the people is not just to 'fill the pews' but it is about drawing in people to find their identity, their place of authority, their seated Heavenly position (as symbolised by the reference to seats). The fact the seats are empty shows that there is space for each one to find their place and their identity in Jesus and in the body of Christ. This is summarised in the following scripture:

> *And God raised us up with Christ and seated us with him in the Heavenly realms in Christ Jesus.* Ephesians 2:6.

Given this context, the dream is what we would categorise as a calling dream. The **$0.50** represents both the number 5 and 50. The number 5 represents Grace (see Chapter 9) and so there is a grace on the dreamer's life for intercession. In addition, the dreamer is able to see and hear in the spirit and know God's timings as they pray. There is a sense of organisation (pews in the Church where in reality there are chairs), and specificity (science link) in these prayers that will help to bring in the people to occupy the empty seats as people find their place and purpose.

There is also a cost and investment to see this happen. The investment from the preacher in the dream symbolises an impartation (investment) from the preacher to release people into an intercession calling but also in a seer anointing to open people's spiritual ears and eyes (audio-visual) to see what is happening in the spirit realm.

This was exciting as the dream was given only a few weeks before my (the preacher in the dream) visit to minister at the Church; what is more I have a seer anointing. The number 5 also reminds us of the parable of the talents (Matthew 25:14-30) where we have to invest (although it does not feel like much, i.e. $0.50). In this case intercession is the investment and then the congregation can anticipate the increased return which is the filling of the empty seats. As people join the volunteer intercession line at the end of the dream, there is an emphasis that everyone's $0.50 is vital at this time. It also reflects that the impartation from the preacher stirs up a hunger in the hearts of people to seek the Lord in prayer for this time and to see people finding faith either for the first time or deepening their existing faith. This celebration is symbolised in the dream by the number 50 which in the Bible represents the year of jubilee that signifies freedom, harvest, joy, restoration, freeing people from slavery and debts (Numbers 36:4 and Leviticus 25:8-50).

As a footnote, I re-visited the church a year later. I found many of the empty seats had indeed been filled as the congregation had engaged in intercession and prayed in people to occupy the seats and discover their place and purpose. This shows that as we steward God's communication to us through dreams, we often see the fruit and practical application in our own lives.

Break open creativity

Chapter 4

YOUR TURN TO INTERPRET A DREAM Part 2 – Complex Dreams

Systematic activation of Chapter 2 teaching

- Three Connected Dreams: Going back to College
- Double Layer Dream: Clear the Chess Board

Three Connected Dreams: Going Back to College

This example, received in 2020 from Australia, is a series of three dreams, which all have the same underlying message. Therefore, here you can practise at trying to interpret each individual dream and then look for the pattern that connects them together with the life principles and application for the dreamer. It is important to remember there is a three-part principle with any word of prophecy or dream which is Revelation, Interpretation and Application. This is covered in depth in my previous book, Speakers of Life, How to Live an Everyday Prophetic Lifestyle (see Chapter 10). The first is the revelation component which is the dream in this case, then there is the interpretation which should lead to an application in the dreamer's life in their words, lifestyle or strategy. With this principle in mind, let's look at the three dreams.

Dream A

I arrive in Oxford and go to the house I am going to be staying at. I am really excited. It is one of those two up two down Victorian houses on a green. I am not quite sure what I'm going to be doing there but I feel a tremendous sense of well-being. I make a coffee in the kitchen and look out the window realising I am home.

Dream B

I'm trying to find my college and go into the nearest one on the high street. The front gate contains the most intricate stone carvings. I walk into the Senior Common Room, nod at a few people and make a coffee. I know I shouldn't be there but I know I belong in Cambridge so it's kind of OK. I finish my coffee and walk out to find my college.

Dream C

I enter the hall at my college – a fantastically detailed painted medieval palace. I start flying around the hall inspecting the ceiling, walls and corners. I come down and fly down a corridor. There is a huge snake waiting for me. I try to run then turn to defend myself as it strikes me hard.

Interpretation: **Dream A**

Here is the interpretation using the three defined steps.

1) **Simplify the Dream,** to three sentences:

- The dreamer was excited to be back in Oxford but not sure of the purpose for being there.
- The dreamer stays in a two up, two down Victorian house on a green.

- Whilst in the kitchen, the dreamer looks out of the window and realises they are home.

2) **Focus**. The dreamer is the focus of the dream because if you take them out of the dream then the dream falls apart.

3) **Context (sub-focus and details):** There are four main points of sub-focus in this dream and these are (in the order that they occur in the dream):

Oxford, Victorian, Green, Window

Taking these in order. This is a going "back to learn things" dream. The name **Oxford** comes from the old term 'Oxanforda' which literally means a ford (shallow crossing) in the river where the cattle (Oxen) could cross safely. Here there is a crossing point involving oxen which in the Bible means Holy Spirit and strength. It fits with Proverbs 14:4 which says:

Where there are no oxen, the manger is empty, but from the strength of an ox come abundant harvests.

This scripture speaks about the future birth of Jesus who was born in a stable or cowshed that would have been full of livestock along with the mess and the smell. Its message is that if we try and sanitise our churches and remove the Holy Spirit (Oxen) then Jesus is no longer there (the manger is empty).

The **Victorian** house is a play on words relating to Victory over the dreamer's house or life. The victory is manifest as increased fruitfulness and this is symbolised by the colour **green** which represents the nine fruits of the Holy Spirit described in the Bible (Galatians 5:22-23).

Finally, the **window** represents increased vision or perspective; a seeing from one realm to another, often to a larger vista which is approaching. This crossing of one realm to another fits with the name of Oxford which is itself representative of a crossing point from one place to another.

Therefore, if we put all these components together, the dreamer is going back to learn anew (or regain what has been lost from years ago) the reality of the Holy Spirit in their life. This will give them strength as well as walking in increased victory and seeing even more fruitfulness in their lives. At the same time, this will enable the dreamer to have a new perspective in their life and to fulfil dreams that were given to them many years earlier in their home in Oxford, as they cross from one place to another more fruitful realm.

Interpretation: **Dream B**

1) **Simplify the Dream,** to three sentences:

- The dreamer is trying to find their college and goes into the nearest one on the High Street through the front gate.
- Even though they are in the wrong place they feel confident as they belong in Cambridge.
- They finish by walking out to find their college.

2) **Focus**. The dreamer is the focus of the dream because if you take them out of the dream then the dream falls apart.

3) **Context (sub-focus and details):** There are four main points of sub-focus in this dream and these are (in the order that they occur in the dream):

High Street, Front Gate, I belong, Cambridge

Taking these in order, this is also a going back dream this time to connect possibly what has been learnt in Dream A. The **High Street** is usually the most visible thoroughfare in a town and the "high" word reinforces the word "visibility" as the higher one climbs the greater is the ability to see more of the surroundings.

The **front gate** is the main entry point and by entering this rather than any side or back gate suggests the dreamer has confidence and is happy to be seen. Even though the dreamer finds that they are in the wrong place they still have enough confidence to stop and have a coffee because they feel **"I belong"** in Cambridge as an entity and not just the college. This confidence can be summed up in the Bible phrase where we see that as children of our Heavenly Father or Papa God that we belong as:

> *we can approach the throne of grace with confidence.* (Hebrews 4:16).

Cambridge means a crossing or bridge over the river Cam. A bridge is a transfer from one place to another or a connection of two places and a river can often mean the Holy Spirit.

Putting all this together, the dreamer is confidently going back to Cambridge to find their college and to connect or bridge to this place of learning in the past, with the work of the Holy Spirit (the river) which will provide and give more visibility to their destiny and calling. As a footnote to this, nothing will be lost as the dreamer has a fine eye for details (intricate stone carvings).

Interpretation: **Dream C**

1) **Simplify the Dream,** to three sentences:

- The dreamer begins to fly around the hall of their college noticing the structural details.
- There is a huge snake waiting for the dreamer in the corridor.
- The snake strikes him as he turns to defend himself.

2) **Focus.** The dreamer is the focus of the dream because if you take them out of the dream then the dream falls apart.

3) **Context (sub-focus and details):** There are four main points

of sub-focus in this dream and these are (in the order that they occur in the dream):

Flying, Corridor, Huge Snake, Defend Myself

Taking these in order, this is also a going back dream to provide strategy relating to dreams A and B. **Flying** is one of the common dream categories and in this case it represents liberty and provides a good perspective enabling the dreamer to see (seer gifting implication here) details which are important to keep things in place (ceilings, walls etc…).

A **corridor** represents transition, connection or crossing like a bridge to a greater level of calling and destiny. In many cases this transition generally represents a good breakthrough which the forces of evil would seek to prevent. As a general spiritual principle, there is often intimidation waiting at the door or corridor of breakthrough and opportunity. This intimidation is presented by a **huge snake** in this dream.

As we describe in Chapter 5, a large snake has a large tail which is a play on words symbolising large amounts of gossip or telling tales. There is therefore a large, coordinated verbal campaign issued against the dreamer to intimidate and frighten them away from their breakthrough at the end of the corridor.

The dreamer runs and then turns to **"defend myself"** but the snake strikes hard. This is an important lesson in tackling snakes (gossip, hostile verbal intimidation) as the best way to avoid the snakes is to keep flying high. Do not abandon the air space and descend to where the snakes are resident as you will get bitten by the gossip. Keep to the high ground. This is very true in the natural world as the frequency of snakes decreases with increasing altitude. The dreamer should therefore have kept flying. We can give them a score of 10 out of 10 for effort, but a low score out of 10 for strategy. In addition, by adopting the wrong strategy, the dreamer receives a bite and ends the dream by running away from their calling and destiny (however they do eventually succeed, see the paragraph below).

This interpretation of dream C can be put together in the light of dreams A and B. The dreamer is clearly having to go back in their lives to learn or re-learn something of the Holy Spirit which is represented in dream A by Oxen and in dream B by a river (the Cam). The dreamer is confident and has every right to be there making this connection or bridge and it causes the dreamer to have greater vision (window, dream A; high, dream B; flying, dream C). The significance of the calling and destiny on this stage of the dreamer's life is exemplified by the degree of opposition, namely the huge snake in dream C. However, despite the fact that the dreamer made the wrong strategy, we see that they did not fall ill or die and we know that ultimately they will achieve victory (Victoria house in Dream A) overcoming the snake and walking in amazing fruitfulness (green in dream A).

Double Layer Dream: Clear the Chess Board

Once again, this is a real example of a dream that was sent in 2020 from the UK during the writing of this book and it has a wide-reaching significance.

> *I had a dream that there was a chess board table with all the pieces and a player sitting there – all of a sudden there was a great force and whoosh the player swept his forearm across the chess board and the pieces went flying, and then the chess board as well. As this happened, I knew the force to be the same as when the money changers and the dove sellers had their tables turned over in the outer courts of the temple (as in the Bible). As this happened, I heard the song come out of the whoosh and it was 'oh the games people play, every night and every day, never meaning what they say, never saying what they mean'. The song goes on to talk about whiling away time in ivory towers, blaming others for things etc. While all this was going on I was immediately listening to the word that the Lord spoke to me loud and clear about a year ago which said 'Knights to*

Kings Cross', and I knew these things were connected.

Here is the interpretation using the three defined steps.
1) **Simplify the Dream**. If we wanted to simplify the dream to three sentences, we would write the following:

- A single chess player with a mighty whoosh swept the pieces off the chess board in a similar fashion to Jesus overturning the tables in the temple courts.
- As this was happening, the dreamer heard a well-known pop song about the games people play and whiling away time in ivory towers.
- Simultaneously the dreamer was reminded of a previous word from God that said 'Knights to Kings Cross'.

2) **Focus**. The chess player (not the dreamer this time) is the focus of the dream because if you take them out of the dream then the dream falls apart.

3) **Context (sub-focus and details):** The dreamer was asked a few questions to clarify the basic principles which were described in Chapter 2 and their reply (in italics) follows the categories described in that chapter.

Strong emotions? *"I felt excitement and joy and also wonder. I felt it was God at the black and white chess board and that was exciting. I seemed to engage well with the dream and was not at all afraid. I felt the emotion of the player was more "anger or frustration" and "I could feel it but it wasn't bad, it felt natural and I felt wonder, like this was how it is supposed to be".*

Colour/Black and White, Day or night?. *"It was colour and it was in the night but I suspect towards morning around 3am".*
The main points of sub-focus in this dream (in the order they appear are):

Chess Board/Pieces, Great Force/Whoosh, Overturning Tables, the Pop Song, Knights to Kings Cross

This is a great dream and has two layers. The first layer I will deal with according to the principles already detailed in Chapter 2. The second layer is a little more advanced and requires a detailed knowledge of the meaning of numbers in dreams (as described in Chapter 9).

First Layer:

The focus is the chess player who the dreamer believes to be God. This is a prophetic dream that speaks of what God is doing and going to do. The black and white **chess board** speaks of the 'game' of religion. In other words, how segments of the church have become positional, imposing rigid black and white structures and black and white rigid thinking on people. The spirit of religion, as opposed to true faith, has controlled the way that people have moved and thought. It has kept them limited, two dimensional in thinking and movement and colourless. Religion is man-made and is defined as that which looks like the truth but has no power. Religion is all about performance to get to God rather than simply accepting Jesus' work on the cross to enjoy access to God's presence.

This reality is reinforced by the **pop song** which speaks of the hypocrisy of parts of the church. Their black and white, positional thinking leads to them playing the 'blame' game. The ivory tower resonates with the *'white washed tombs'* of the Pharisees described in the Bible (Matthew 23:27), who look righteous on the outside but are dead on the inside.

God is **overturning the tables** as he did in the outer courts of the temple (John 2:15). He is shaking the whole system including the Bishops and all the religious **(chess) pieces**. Furthermore, even the paradigms of thought, structure and hierarchy will be overthrown and turned upside down. The lesser kings (chess pieces) or gods of society shall diminish in influence. God is angry about the religion that he sees as this is not blessing or loving the people. Instead religion is containing them. The creator God exists outside of these paradigms and cannot be contained or controlled.

The great force or whoosh speaks of a 'suddenly' move of the Holy Spirit, who is the breath of God. As God dismantles the limitations of man-made religion and church, he is calling his **knights**, men and women and children of nobility (the Bible tells us we are a Royal Priesthood, 1 Peter 2:9) to rally once more to the cross of their King Jesus, who is the King of Kings **(i.e. Kings Cross).** As opposed to any man-made religion, the Kings Cross is once again raised up as the standard of the church as Jesus is the true gospel and the life path we take as we follow our King and lift him high. The movement or rallying to **Kings Cross** links with the Bible scripture in John 12:32:

> *'And I when I am lifted up from the earth, will draw all people to myself'.*

In addition, the way that knights move on a chessboard are unique and not obvious. They are the only pieces that do not move in a straight line and they can jump over obstacles. This speaks to a spiritual context, a searching out of things which are not obvious, to find those hidden treasures of God beyond the obstacle in the way. This links in with the following verse in the Proverbs 25:2:

> *It is the glory of Kings to search the matter out.*

Here there is an intentional play on words with Kings in the above scripture and **Kings Cross** in the dream. It is the sacrifice of King Jesus on the Cross that gives us access to God. This is in contrast to human efforts, performance and actions which do not work and are symbolic of religion rather than true faith in God through Jesus. If this is not true in your life, and you have been following religion rather than Jesus, then a prayer to help you make this a reality is on the first page of Chapter 10.

Second Layer

If we delve a little deeper there is a second layer to the dream partly involving numbers which are not explicitly recounted by the dreamer. This is where the "revelation is given" part of dream interpretation takes centre stage. Incidentally this second layer of interpretation resonated very deeply when it was shared with the dreamer. In addition, the process of revealing these two layers of the dream was greatly facilitated by the interpretation process being undertaken by a team of two people, myself and Natasha (who is credited in the preface).

There is an important principle here, which is that one can always learn from others by working as a team and also that it helps to bounce certain questions off someone else for accountability purposes and rigour. This principle is relevant not only when you are learning but also when you have some years of interpretation under your belt. This second layer of interpretation used the first layer as a springboard for the revelation process which secondarily involved the skill process of knowing the meaning of the numbers (remember- **skill is acquired, revelation is given**).

Here then is the second layer of the dream: The chess pieces are meant to be connected to the board and vice versa. The chess pieces follow a strategy defined by the context of the board. However, when the board becomes limiting, controlling and religious (see layer 1 above) then this affects the strategy of the way that the chess figures (the people in the Church) move around. The solution is that they need to be freed and separated from the board (as in the dream), reset and then reconnected to a board that has a life strategy as opposed to a controlling religious strategy.

Here is the numerical explanation of this scenario: A chess board is made up of a 8x8 set of squares which gives a total of 64 separate squares. Ideally, this represents a template or strategy for new beginnings because the number eight means new beginnings in the Bible (see Chapter 9). It should also represent a strategy for Heavenly spiritual government because if you multiply 6 and 4 together you get 24 which refers to the 24 elders in the Heavenly government in the book of Revelation in the Bible.

In addition, the chess board should not be two-dimensional and limiting but three-dimensional (3D) which speaks of 8+8+8 which is also 24. Therefore, God wants us to have 3D strategy and thinking, with governmental application and authority that has a Heavenly quality. The spirit of religion is totally counter to this and wants us to have two-dimensional thinking in black and white, following a set of rules which have the essence of something but without the power. This is represented in the two-dimensional chess board where if we add the 6 and 4, rather than multiplying the numbers, we make 10 rather than 24. The number 10 represents the rules (the 10 commandments of the law in the Bible) and a focus on this produces performance and religion (see Chapter 9).

In summary, the interpretation of this dream received in 2020 fits well with the 2020 prophetic narrative which speaks of 'new being new' and it being 'far better to be an amateur in the new rather than an expert in the old' (quote from Emma Stark, Glasgow Prophetic Centre and British Isles Council of Prophets). God has to separate the chess figures from the board to reset and place them back not on the same board, which was old and restrictive (number 10), but on a new board which is 3D and is new (8) and governmental (24).

This is so exciting and is of national significance because if acted upon it will change, for the better, the spiritual climate of a nation.

Chapter 5

THE MOST COMMON DREAM CATEGORIES Part 2

- Falling
- Don't Look Down, I'm Flying
- Cleansing Dreams
- Dying
- Snakes and Other Creatures
- Water
- Relatives
- Time
- Storms and Weather
- Activation

Falling

These dreams may have a positive or a negative connotation depending upon the context. On the negative side, they can reveal a fear of losing control of some area of your life. Sometimes the dream may also feature your teeth falling out as this is linked to losing a grip on the situation (see Chapter 1). On the positive side, they can reveal that you are becoming free from something that is restrictive, and you are falling from this into something that may represent freedom and love. Therefore, the scenario or type of substance that you are falling into may be important in the understanding of the dream.

The dominant emotions in the dream will help you to discern

whether you are fearful of losing control or feeling relief and happiness that you are falling into a safe environment from one that was restrictive or harmful. For example, falling from a controlling relationship into the safe ocean of God's love.

Don't Look Down, I'm Flying

Flying dreams often symbolise your ability or potential (either in the physical or spiritual realm) to rise above problems and difficulties. In a spiritual context, flying represents soaring into the Heavenly realm to seek a higher perspective. Moreover, it says in the Bible that we are seated with Christ Jesus in Heavenly places far above all principalities and powers (Ephesians 2:6). What a great view on life!

These types of dreams are some of the most inspirational and encouraging as shown by the fact that when you wake you often feel exhilarated.

Cleansing Dreams

The most common cleansing dream features either sitting in the bathtub, taking a shower, going to the toilet or similar. The dreams are revealing things that are in the process of being washed from you or flushed out of your life. These types of dreams are often good as they symbolise a process or season where, for example, certain grimy thought patterns or disturbing scenarios are being washed off you so that you are no longer affected by them.

This can be either emotionally, psychologically or spiritually. The Bible speaks often about the refreshing rain of Heaven (Isaiah 45:8), being washed in the blood of Jesus (Hebrews 10:22) and being cleansed by washing with the word of God (Ephesians 5:26). All of this deals with the hurt, grime, sickness, or sadness of life both in the past, present and future. It is like having a spiritual Teflon coating where none of the bad stuff sticks.

Dying

We have covered birthing in part 1 of common dream categories (Chapter 1). Clearly the opposite of birthing is dying. As with birthing dreams, those about dying are not normally literally about the person who might be the main focus in the dream.

The dying event is usually symbolic about something that is ending or departing from the dreamer's life. The context, of course, will inform as to whether this is a positive or negative thing. It might be important that there is closure of a season of work, church life, relationships or a community role, simply because things have run their natural course. Alternatively, it might be that all objectives for the dreamer have been met and it is time to move on and perhaps it is time for a new person to take over for the next phase.

The 'knowing when to move on' is quite an important life principle in the community, church or marketplace. This is important for two reasons. Firstly, it is important to realise the timing of seasons in our lives. For example, we may have been fruitful in setting up or maintaining something (possibly for many years) but there comes a moment where the grace or ease for that season has ended. This is because there is something else that we need to move on to, where there is that same ease or grace to operate in and to be inherently fruitful. People can tend to look back rather than let go and be willing to let something die. However, letting go of the 'old thing' they were doing, or passing it onto someone else, allows the person to move onto the next stage of their destiny and also allows life to be breathed back into something that has probably become very stale.

The second reason is that the person who has the ease and grace to take what you are currently doing on to the next glorious level is not able to step into their destiny because you are still occupying that space. This results in additional frustration where the newcomer cannot express themselves in that new role because the current occupier has not moved on, even though they have already become stale and are themselves frustrated and demotivated with how difficult it has all become.

The final comment on this aspect of dying is that the type of death may be important to note in the dream. For example, watch to see if there is resurrection on the other side of the dying process, either biblically (the death and resurrection of Jesus) or the rising from the ashes such as the fable of the phoenix. In this context it is interesting to note that the name of the city 'Atlanta' in the USA has links to a native American name which means 'rising from the ashes' as this is actually what happened historically.

Snakes and Other Creatures

Dreams about snakes are not only one of the most common category of animal dreams, they are one of the most common dreams in any category. Snakes are not a healthy sign in a dream as they represent gossip or someone bad-mouthing you to others. There is a play on words operating here, as snakes of course have a long tail and another phrase for gossip is that people are telling tales about you. Small snakes have small tails and so this represents gossip whereas a large snake has a large tail that represents a more deliberate program of bad-talk perhaps by a group or syndicate of people or organisation.

In spiritual biblical terms, these dreams reveal the serpent in the garden of Eden; this represents the devil at work through accusation, deception, etc. In this context, dreams about snakes coming out of the mouth can symbolise the need for spiritual deliverance of a demonic influence that has been affecting the way the person has been talking, often against their own wishes. I have personally come across this quite a few times when ministering at different churches.

Other animals which symbolise that someone is opening their big mouth about you are, of course, reptiles such as alligators and crocodiles for the obvious reason that they have big mouths compared to their bodies. Sharks often resemble a lack of peace, as in the natural they have to keep swimming otherwise they would drown. Therefore, as a result they are forever roaming and moving, never settling.

Spiders and bears are common in dreams that symbolise fear.

The spider reflects situations where the person is trapped in a web that has been woven in advance for the very intention of catching and harming them, often by injecting its deadly poison. As a result, spiders in dreams are often a symbol of the occult or witchcraft where involved people or demons are trying to trap and harm you.

Of course, this is quite a disturbing dream and may end up as a nightmare. However, it is possible to deal with this whilst experiencing the dream (see also the section on lucid dreams in Chapter 6). We can safely say that the source of a dream featuring spiders is the demonic and darkness, and therefore the solution to this issue is to invite Jesus, who is known also as the light of the world, into your dream to deal with the spiders. Try it whenever spiders come in your dreams and the frequency of those dreams will quickly diminish.

In the natural realm, one would kill a spider by stamping on it, so if there is a spiritually evil element to the dream then the solution is to stamp on the spiders with our spiritual feet which, according to the Bible, are fitted with peace (Ephesians 6:15). Therefore, inviting Jesus into our dream is a spiritual way of changing our bad dreams into a blessing, a big loss into a big win!

After the occurrence of snakes in a dream the most common animal to appear is the dog. The meaning of this symbolism depends upon context. On the positive side, a dog can indicate friendship, loyalty and protection whereas on the negative side a dog can indicate attacking, biting, fear. The term that "a dog is a man's best friend" can be relevant in the dream as it could reveal a friend who is about to betray you or conversely someone who is going to become a real trusted friend.

Vermin such as mice, rats and cockroaches etc. often carry a negative connotation in a dream. This is because in the natural there is an increase in vermin where there is unattended garbage. Therefore, in dream language, the occurrence of vermin can symbolise that there are things have not been attended to in your life. In other words, if these things are neglected then they will attract vermin. The solution therefore is to "clean up our act". If there is nothing to attract the vermin then they will not come and feed off the garbage in our lives.

In the spiritual context, vermin can represent the demonic realm which is attracted to "garbage" behaviour and unhealthy, habitual thought patterns in our lives. The spiritual solution or antidote to this overlaps with the principles found in cleansing dreams which we have already covered, such as the blood of Jesus and the washing by the Word of God. This is a spiritual solution to a spiritual problem which, if left unattended, can manifest as a physical problem. This scenario can be seen in all walks of life and buildings including churches. For example, I was involved in anointing the inside of a church building with oil and declaring the blood of Jesus to clean up a church from gossip and the spirit of control which had attracted demonic attention.

All of the animals and creatures described above can also appear as white versions. If the symbol of the animal is evil, then the white nature represents an additional layer of the religious spirit. This is akin to white witchcraft or white lies where it appears that just because it is white it is more acceptable. However, the truth is that lies are lies whatever colour or shade you try and dress them.

If the animal or creature is already positive, then a version of that animal which is covered in light or emanates light, thereby appearing white, may enhance the purity or holy aspect of that symbol. Conversely if the animal is an evil creature then the white simply represents a poor counterfeit of goodness, holiness and purity.

Water

Water is usually a positive symbol in a dream. In a spiritual context, water has its origins in the river of life as mentioned in the Bible in the book of Revelation, where not only is there life but also healing along the banks of the river. Going deeper in a river or water is seen as a good thing and is often linked to the river of God flowing from the temple described in Ezekiel 47:1-12. The reader is encouraged to go deeper and be immersed in water, to take their feet off the bottom so that their path is governed by the flow of the river of God.

Being underwater or submerged can represent the deep things of the Spirit. For example, in another place in the Bible (Psalm 42), the reader is encouraged to go deep with God and for his waves to break over you. This is a picture in which it is better to be overwhelmed by the love of God than by being overwhelmed with work, stress, jealousy, bullying, fear, unkindness etc.

Therefore, it is not surprising in a biblical spiritual context that water and rivers usually represent the Holy Spirit, aspects of spiritual life and moves of God's activity in your own life or communities or the land. Larger bodies of water such as oceans often represent the mass of humanity.

Relatives

In most cases, these dreams indicate generational issues at work in your life, this can be positive or negative, a blessing or a curse. This requires a degree of discernment as it is always good to accept a blessing whilst at the same time being able to identify a curse and cut off its influence upon you along the generational lines. A clear indication of generational issues, good or bad, is the occurrence of grandparents appearing in your dreams.

Then there are dreams where you meet someone you have never met before. This stranger may be threatening you, which of course is a warning dream. Alternatively, they may be sent to help you in a constructive manner, in which case this dream is to give you foreknowledge, to alert you in order to identify the help. Usually if you cannot see the face of the helper, then it is an angel (or the Holy Spirit) but if you see some facial details then it is likely to be a person you will meet in the future. Even if you only have some facial details, you will have a "feel" for the nature of that person so that when you do meet them you will have a sense that you have met them before and can act accordingly.

For example, in 2018, I was praying with a group of people from different churches along the Mason-Dixon line which stretches along the border of Maryland and Pennsylvania in the USA. It involved meeting a key person from a local church near the Mason-Dixon line. I had never met them before, and it was going to be important to be able to trust them very quickly. I arrived at the approximate location and began to look around to see which of the strangers that I could see was the right one. About seventy yards away I saw someone sitting on a bench and they had a familiar "feel" about them which reminded me of a very helpful stranger I had met in a dream some six months earlier. As I approached the person their facial details confirmed exactly the person I had met in my dream. Yes indeed, it was THE person that I needed to meet from the local church in that area. I shared my story with the person, and they'd had a similar experience in a dream or vision about 6 months earlier as well. This meant that mutual trust was cemented from the get-go!

As an aside, that very morning of the visit to the Mason-Dixon line I'd had a very clear intense emotional vision in full colour about Jesus walking on the battlefield near the Mason-Dixon line during the American civil war. In this vision, Jesus was being so tender with each of the dead and dying soldiers as they lay alone amongst the horror of war and he was describing the places and mansions prepared for them in Heaven. This vision was also connected to a dream of mine focussed on the everlasting life in Jesus for these soldiers in Heaven. I had forgotten about all of this until, during the writing of this book, an American friend sent me a copy of *My Dream of Heaven* (Springer, 1898) written just after the American Civil war in the 19th century. This 1898 book details a vivid dream of Heaven including the exact details of the very same mansions I had previously seen in my vision. There was a great deal of overlap with my vision and dream some one hundred and twenty years later after the book was written. This speaks of the fact that the spiritual realm of Heaven is not bound by time.

Time

Speaking of time, even though the Heavenly realm is "outside of time" it is important to notice when Heaven breaks through into our physical domain and chronologic time. Clocks or watches in a dream can represent the need for a wake-up call for either the dreamer or possibly an organisation, region or nation depending upon the context of the dream.

Alternatively, time can represent what time it is in your life or it might be a time for the dreamer to be alert and watchful. The example in the Bible is a lookout or watcher on the walls of the city. These dreams may indicate a Scripture verse as well, giving a deeper message. For example, being woken at 5.25am may be an encouragement to keep in step, pace or in time with the Holy Spirit as mentioned in Galatians 5:25.

Storms and Weather

What kind of storm is it? Are there tornadoes involved, as these can indicate a change in life or circumstances that is coming? This may be good or bad depending on the context, as tornadoes can indicate great destruction. Storm dreams usually tend to hint at things that are on the horizon. This can be good or bad such as refreshment to a dry land or destructive storms. These types of dreams are particularly common for people who have a gift or calling in the area of seeing and discernment of what is to come, whether it is good or bad, and who then know what to do about it (termed an Issachar gift in 1 Chronicles 12:32). In spiritual terms, these dreamers are likely to be seers particularly in the area of spiritual warfare. Discernment is key because if you see a whirlwind in a dream it is not necessarily bad because we read in Nahum 1:3 that God's way is in the whirlwind.

In the spiritual context the colour is important. For example, storms which are light in colour can be from God, whereas dark storms can represent evil and turbulence in life. Winds can be positive, such as being pushed or blown by the Holy Spirit in our journey, or negative, representing adversity such as when we try to run or perhaps sail metaphorically into the wind.

The rain can often represent a spiritual blessing from Heaven of refreshment or an episode of emotional, spiritual or physical cleansing that is approaching. If the rain is dirty rain or acid rain (e.g. pollution) then it represents a destructive or evil episode that may be coming your way.

Earthquakes usually represent judgment or shaking. It is also important to understand that just because you experience something in a dream then it is not a fait accompli. On the contrary, it provides an opportunity for us to position ourselves either to be helped by the weather condition or to avoid it. For example, to get in the way of helpful weather would result in being refreshed, blown in the right direction along our journey or obstacles being ripped out of our way. Dodging harmful weather would entail getting out of the way of strength sapping head winds and avoiding the destruction of what we have built.

The Bible references are:

Storms: Psalm 107: 25-29; Isaiah 25:4; Psalm 83:14-15.

Tornadoes (whirlwinds): Nahum 1:3; Ezekiel 1:4; Jeremiah 25:32; Jeremiah 30:23.

Winds: Isaiah 32:2; Ezekiel 13:13; Genesis 8:1; Isaiah 40:24.

Earthquakes: Luke 21:11; Mark 13:8; Revelation 11:13; Acts 16:26.

Rain: Isaiah 45:8; Isaiah 55:10; Jeremiah 5:24; Joel 2:23; Matthew 5:45.

Activation

Please take the opportunity to categorise your dreams if they fall into the common categories in this chapter or in Chapter 1. This will help you to see if there any repetitive patterns or links between your dreams.

If there are certain dreams within the same category, it suggests that a certain principle, issue or relationship is being highlighted and needs attention in your life.

Calling, Destiny and Purpose

I AM with you always

Free to be me!

Prayer of a righteous man!

Let it rain

Safest place in the world!!

She Can Scale The Wall

Vision

Chapter 6

DREAMS AND SLEEP

- The Science of Sleep and Remembering Dreams
- Preparing for Dreams
- Activation 1: Begin with Rest
- Activation 2: Work from Rest

The Science of Sleep and Remembering Dreams

The Oxford English Dictionary defines dreams as "a series of images, events and feelings that happen in your mind while you are asleep". Dreams mainly occur in the rapid-eye movement (REM) stage of sleep. However, there has been evidence in the Journal of Sleep Research (Takeuchi, 2001) showing that a minor proportion of dreams are associated with the non-rapid eye movement (NREM) although the dreams occurring in NREM seem to be less vivid and memorable (Hobson, 2009).

REM sleep is manifest by continuous movements of the eyes during sleep and it occurs when brain activity is high, resembling the scenario that occurs when the individual is awake. Infants spend more time in REM sleep than adults and the proportion of REM sleep then decreases significantly through childhood. Older people in general tend to sleep less overall, but they sleep in REM for about the same absolute time. This means that older people spend a greater proportion of sleep in REM (Markov et.al, 2012).

REM sleep episodes and the dreams that accompany them lengthen progressively throughout the night and during a full eight-hour night sleep, most dreams occur in the typical two hours of REM. The first episode of REM is the shortest and typically lasts for approximately 10-12 minutes. The second and third episodes increase to a typical duration of approximately 15-20 minutes. The length of a dream varies, lasting for a few seconds to approximately 20-30 minutes (Hobson, 2009). Dreams tend to last longer as the night progresses; the average person has three to five dreams per night, and some may even have up to seven (Empson, 2002), however it is typical that most dreams are immediately or quickly forgotten.

People are more likely to remember the dream if they wake during the REM phase. Typically, control individuals (i.e. not on medication etc.) can report a dream 50% of the time if they are woken before they have reached the end of their first REM period. This retrieval rate is increased to more than 95% when individuals are woken during the last REM period of the night (Takeuchi, 2005).

Certain techniques can help increase dream recall. Anything that captures our attention immediately after waking can interfere with the efficiency of dream recall. This is because it is thought that as the brain awakens, it starts to turn on processes needed for long-term storage. Therefore, if we wake straight out of a dream, there is a greater probability of remembering it. Studies have shown that greater 'theta' brain-wave activity in the prefrontal cortex after waking from REM sleep enhances dream recall (Hutchison and Rathmore, 2015). Theta activity can be described as low frequency oscillations in the local field potential within the parts of the brain called the hippocampus, amygdala and neocortex. Theta activity indicates a slower-paced, more relaxed brain state, and greater theta activity has been linked to enhanced memory while awake (see below about preparing for sleep).

Therefore, try to keep a notepad and pen, recording device or smartphone by the bed or if you are going to sleep on a long-haul flight for example. When you first wake up, do not jump up or turn your attention to something, as often the simple discipline of beginning to write down or record your dream will enhance the recall of the rest of the dream. It is like the process of crossing a river using stepping stones when there is a mist over the water. You can see enough of the first one to step on it and then once you have done that then the second one comes into view and so on. Even if you do not think you can remember a dream, take just a minute to see if there is any feeling or image you can describe which may cause an entire dream to come flooding back. If you wait until after you brush your teeth or comb your hair to ask this question, you will have already forgotten many of your dreams.

Always date your dream and note where you were and when you received it and also try to give the dream a summary title. This helps to categorise your dreams and highlights any repetitive patterns that may occur in dreams over a period of time. It is amazing how much our dream life increases once we begin the discipline of keeping a notebook and pen or smartphone close to our bed to record our dreams. The process of recording our dreams also shows that we value what these dreams are saying to us. If we believe that God is speaking to us in dreams, then it shows that we treasure these spiritual parables of the night. In the Bible, where dreams are documented throughout the entire book, a prophet called Habakkuk writes in Habakkuk 2:2 about proper recording:

> *Write down the revelation and make it plain on tablets.*

Little did Habbakuk know that in speaking about tablets he was foretelling the invention of iPads and Samsung tablets (sorry, couldn't help that joke!!!). In 1 Chronicles we see that King David valued the process of recording what God said:

> *All this I have in writing as a result of the Lord's hand on me.*
> (1 Chronicles 28:19).

Before we think about how what we do before sleep has an impact on our dreams, it is worth being aware of the two common sleep mechanisms.

These are internal biological mechanisms called circadian rhythms and sleep-wake cycle or homeostasis (i.e. maintaining an internal physiological balance). Both mechanisms work together to regulate when we are awake and sleep.

Circadian rhythms direct a wide variety of functions ranging from daily fluctuations in wake duration to body temperature, metabolism, and the release of hormones. They control the timing of your sleep, being sleepy at night and the tendency to wake in the morning without an alarm. The biological clock of your body is based on a roughly 24-hour day and it controls most circadian rhythms. Circadian rhythms synchronize with light, temperature and other environmental cues during the day, but they continue even in the absence of cues.

The sleep-wake homeostasis reminds the body to sleep after a certain time and regulates sleep intensity. The drive gets stronger every hour you are awake and causes you to sleep longer and more deeply after a period of sleep deprivation. Factors that influence your sleep-wake cycle include medical conditions, medications, stress, sleep environment, what you eat and drink and also light exposure. This is why exposure to light can make it difficult to fall asleep and return to sleep when awakened. There have been many studies on night shift workers who often have trouble falling asleep when they go to bed, and also have trouble staying awake at work due to disruption of their natural circadian rhythm and sleep-wake cycle.

In the case of jet lag, circadian rhythms become out of synchrony with the time of day when people fly to a different time zone. This creates a lack of match in timing or "lag" between their internal clock and the actual clock of the time zone in the country they are visiting.

Preparing for Dreams

Here are some tips for preparing to receive dreams but also being open to dreams from the right source, in other words, good dreams rather than nightmares (see Chapter 7).

1). In the light of the scientific advantages of rest on our dreams as described above, try to develop an evening bedtime routine that encourages rest and peace. The Bible says:

> *The peace of God which transcends all understanding, will guard your hearts and your minds in Christ Jesus.* (Philippians 4:7).

Therefore, it makes sense to give permission for the God of Peace to give you dreams, even to be in these dreams, and to focus on the peace of God rather than destructive things before going to sleep.

2). This leads on to the issue of being mindful of the focus of your senses especially before you go to sleep. What you listen to or watch will also affect your mind and thought patterns. TV is a classic dream snatcher; therefore avoid going to bed straight from the television or even falling asleep while watching TV.

It says in the Bible to focus on things that are right, pure, and praiseworthy for a good reason (Philippians 4:8). Relaxing with words like this in the Bible, or listening to worship music, are examples of these healthy inputs that can be the last things our mind is conscious of before going to sleep.

Try to avoid peace snatchers such as addictions and unhealthy life patterns affecting your mind, will and emotions; these will only breed unforgiveness, bitterness, worry and anger. In fact, the Bible tells us not to go to sleep angry because of the way it breeds and broods in us overnight, including having adverse effects on our dreams (Ephesians 4:26).

3). Develop the skill of "Lucid Dreaming". This is where even though you are in a dream you have the ability to interact with it, but at the same time think independently from your dream. This process is greatly heightened, and much safer spiritually, if we invite the God of Heaven, Jesus and the Holy Spirit into our dreams not just while they are happening but also before we fall asleep. This approach makes sense if we believe that dreams are a means of communicating with Heaven and the God of Heaven.

A few examples of lucid dreaming are: asking questions in the dream, asking for the interpretation as you are dreaming and also changing the ending of the dream. The advantage of lucid dreaming is that when you are interacting in this way you increase the detail retention of the dream plus you tend to wake up already interacting with God about your dream. As all true revelation belongs to God, then asking God will help us not only with dream retention and knowing what the dreams mean but also with what we should do about it.

A great example of a lucid dream is the account of King Solomon who arguably was the wisest King on record. King Solomon clearly interacted with God in the dream and was asked what he wanted. He chose wisdom rather than other choices of riches, long life or defeat of his enemies. As a result, he got his first choice of incredible wisdom having no equal in his lifetime. He even received the other choices of riches, long life and battle victories because he had the wisdom to know how to administer them in his life and kingdom (1 Kings 3:5-15).

It may seem a little presumptive to some reading this book that we can communicate with the creator of the universe in our dreams. It only makes sense when we realise that we are daughters and sons of the living creator God and that he wants to continually pour out limitless buckets of love over us every second of every day and night (1 John 3:1). We have access to God because of the sacrifice of Jesus, which additionally defeated and disarmed all evil powers. Therefore, it is not surprising that many people have reported taking the invitational outstretched hand of Jesus in their dreams to solve and deal with traumas and harmful events or nightmare scenarios.

4). Evidence has suggested, where possible, to plan to wake up gently and slowly which will mean avoiding loud jarring alarm clocks and trying softer methods such as gentle music e.g. worship music.

5). Take a few moments before you get out of bed to reflect on whether you had any dreams that night, even a glimmer. If that is the case, then intentionally think on the fragment of that dream for a few moments and try to complete a full recall and write it down or record it before you get out of bed. Even if it is only a small detail, please value it and treasure it. The Bible talks about not despising the day of small beginnings, as this prepares us to receive more (Zechariah 4:10).

During the process of recall, be mindful of distractions that may interrupt this process and thereby threaten to decrease the recall. This will be different for each person and may only appear tiny and insignificant but might be highly effective in ruining the recall. In fact, the Bible talks about this principle where it says beware of those *"little foxes that may ruin the vineyard"* in Song of Songs 2:15.

Activation 1: Begin with Rest

We have touched briefly on the scientific and spiritual advantages of rest and dreams as described in the above sections of this chapter. In his book on dreams (2006), James Goll states that "rest is the incubation of revelation". God rested from the work of creation on the seventh day and Jesus urged us to find rest by coming to him and letting him carry our yoke in exchange for the one from him that will provide rest:

> *Come to me, all you who are weary and burdened, and I will give you rest. Take my yoke upon you and learn from me, for I am gentle and humble in heart, and you will find rest for your souls. For my yoke is easy and my burden is light* (Matthew 11:28-30).

Therefore, as an activation exercise, it really makes sense to dream from a place of rest and to prepare for your dreams from a place of rest. Instead of the well-known term "hitting the ground running", we are hitting the dream ground resting. This place of rest then becomes a safe, secure and restoring springboard to take off and soar in our dreams. If we want Heavenly dreams, then we have to focus on Heavenly rest.

One part of this activation of beginning with rest is to follow the advice of the scripture above and to offload to Jesus all the burdens of the day that would wear us out and rob us of our peace. The peace of God that we read about earlier in Philippians 4:6-7, is closely linked to the process of getting rid of anxiety. This process effectively makes more room in our inner being for peace to flood our hearts and mind. The Passion Translation of these verses puts it so well:

> *Don't be pulled in different directions or worried about a thing. Be saturated in prayer throughout each day, offering your faith-filled requests before God with overflowing gratitude. Tell him every detail of your life, then God's wonderful peace that transcends human understanding, will make the answers known to you through Jesus Christ.* (Philippians 4:6-7 TPT).

There are clearly two parts to this activation: part 1 is getting rid of the anxiety by handing it over to Jesus, and part 2 is to accept from Jesus the flooding of your heart and mind with perfect peace straight from Heaven. This is the perfect activation exercise for connecting with Heaven through your dreams.

I know some of you will be thinking "I'm not sure about all this passive rest stuff because I have so many obstacles and battles to overcome each day". Well interestingly in the days of the Old Testament, there was a famous mighty warrior called Josheb-Basshebeth (2 Samuel 23:8) whose name literally means "dwelling in rest"! In the 21st century, we may not be confronted with daily physical battles and the danger of an enemy that may overwhelm us, but we are confronted by a myriad of skirmishes and battles (psychologically, spiritually, physically and emotionally) that would seek to overwhelm us and rob us of our peace, hope and love. Therefore, let us win these modern battles and live a lifestyle of an overcomer as we "dwell in rest".

Two good questions to ask at this point are:

- How do we dwell in rest?
- What are the fruits of dwelling in rest?

The answer to the first question is to sow our presence into the presence of God who is the source of all peace. As we repeatedly spend time with someone, we get to recognise their voice above the surrounding and competing noise. In science, this is called maximising the signal to noise ratio so that we can pick up a clear signal against the background interfering noise. Consider how powerful and transforming it would be if we spent more time focussing on the signal of God of Heaven, the creator of the universe who is the source of all peace and rest.

Some of the steps described earlier in preparing for dreams such as listening to worship music, reading the Bible, etc. are simply tuning into him. This 'intentional activation' has been termed 'resting' or 'soaking' in God's presence and it is characterised by a lack of striving and drivenness. The presence of God is where we belong, where we fit, as we are the right spiritual shape (see Chapter 7). This is because it is part of our inheritance as daughters and sons of the living God (1 John 3:1).

The answer to the second question is deeply connected with the fact that as children of God; we are heirs of God through Jesus as it says in the Bible:

> *Now we're no longer living like slaves under the law, but we enjoy being God's very own sons and daughters! And because we're his, we can access everything our Father has – for we are heirs of God through Jesus, the Messiah!* (Galatians 4:7 TPT).

The fruit of this inheritance is something that we do not have to rent or take out a loan to pay for, because Jesus by shedding his blood on the cross has paid the price, settled the cost and it has become legally binding. An inheritance is linked to our identity as God's children who cares for us so much that he sent his son to die for us. This inheritance represents a place of true intimacy, a place of freedom and liberty, where our mind and body are put back together, reshaped and renewed, an amazing upgrade. A place where we are added to and not taken away from by the demands of others wanting a piece of us. A place where we exchange our weariness and the baggage of our lives for peace and rest. It is a place where our ears are tuned in and we only hear the love songs of our Heavenly Father singing over us (Zephaniah 3:17), where our ears are tuned out and do not hear criticism, gossip or any other destructive talk or sound.

Experiencing this frequency of Heaven, from God as our true Father and just like Jesus did, will change our lives. As a child of God, we have access to feel, know, and experience the unconditional, extravagant, intimate love of our Heavenly Father or 'Abba' as the Bible expresses this relationship which translated from the Hebrew means 'Daddy' or 'Papa'.

This activation exercise 1, which begins with rest, represents a challenge for many people as they find it is easier to "do" than "be", particularly in the 21st century where we can "do" a lot from our own space or home. We need to be intentional in creating space in our lives to simply be, it is almost like ring fencing or safeguarding the time. I simply post it into my work diary so that people cannot "book" that time with me and inadvertently steal it.

Once we begin to experience the numerous benefits of resting or soaking in the presence of God's love such as identity, acceptance, peace, healing, wholeness, freedom and more, then this will increasingly motivate us to safeguard those times in our weekly diary. Once this pattern is established, it will become a lifestyle choice like going to the gym, a daily walk, exercise and so on. It will become a habit that we do not want to miss. A daily lifestyle (this also means during the night in our dreams) of being constantly filled with the love of God will help us to help others as it is impossible to give away what you have not received.

Through being connected daily to the source of life (Psalm 1:3, John 15:7) we cannot help but speak life and exude life. This will have an enormous effect on the environment around us. For example, take the example of Queen Esther in the Bible. There were many details in the story but an intentional and disciplined process which involved soaking in perfume and essential oils for twelve months led to Esther being chosen as the Royal Queen. The result of this process was that she found herself being in exactly the right place in terms of influence at the right time to save her nation during exile in a foreign land. There is more detail on the principle and process of changing our environment for the better in the following chapters on divine Love (Chapters 7 and 8).

Activation 2: Work from Rest

Once we have begun in rest, the next challenge is to keep in rest and make it a lifestyle so that we do all our activities, including work, from this place of sacred love, peace and rest. It can be a paradigm shift for many as they discover the secret of **working from rest as opposed to resting from work**. Part of the key here is realising that our Heavenly father, papa, dad has our very best interests at heart. He has already made plans in advance to help us with walking out our destiny, calling and purpose in life.

For example, in The Passion Translation:

> *You've gone into my future to prepare the way, and in kindness you follow behind me to spare me from the harm of my past. With your hand of love upon my life, you impart a blessing to me. This is just too wonderful, deep, and incomprehensible!* (Psalm 139:5-6 TPT).

Wow, this means that the creator of the universe has got our backs (i.e. the past), as he walks with us (the present) into the amazing plans he has for us (the future). What is more, he is doing all of this for us whilst we are continually wrapped up in the garments and folds of his love, as we read in the following two scriptures:

> *His massive arms are wrapped around you, protecting you. You can run under his covering of majesty and hide. His arms of faithfulness are a shield keeping you from harm.* (Psalm 91:4 TPT).

> *Every spiritual blessing in the Heavenly realm has already been lavished upon us as a love gift from our wonderful Heavenly Father, the Father of our Lord Jesus – all because he sees us wrapped into Christ. This is why we celebrate him with all our hearts!* (Ephesians 1:3 TPT).

It is so amazing and incomprehensible that all we have to do is to accept and rest in the spiritual reality described in these scriptures and in doing so we can work from REST rather than rest from WORK. The key is to choose and occupy the correct position in the Heavenly realm and apply it in our lives to see the amazing fruit. This correct positioning in the Heavenly realm produces an alignment which prepares us for the assignment we are purposed to do.

It is, however, tempting to do it the other way around where the assignment or the 'doing' precedes and tries to dictate to the alignment or 'being'. This well-meaning but ultimately flawed approach may start well as we seem to accomplish quite a bit in our own strength, but it always finishes badly. This is because we find that we cannot sustain that which we have started, we run out of energy, and run out of vision which steals our joy and thereby makes us feel at best grumpy. All this happens because if we embark on assignment before the alignment then we often have no Heavenly vision or plan.

If we begin with alignment by being and resting in the Heavenly place of rest and love then the vision arising from these times is Heavenly resourced and guarantees that we complete our assignment with strength, purpose and joy (a grumpy free zone!) A useful visual aid for this correct positioning is to picture yourself sitting in one of two chairs which signify different priorities. Chair 1 has the priority of BEING whereas Chair 2 has the priority of DOING. Remember, we are a human BEING not a human DOING. If we drill down a little more, Chair 1 is the place of REST and Alignment where we work from REST. Chair 2, on the other hand is the place of Assignment where we rest from WORK.

Here are some key points, which, when integrated into our daily walk, will produce an abundance of life around us not only in our environment but also in the way we can influence our atmosphere. Not surprisingly, I encourage us all to spend each day living and dwelling from Chair 1 (C1) as opposed to Chair 2 (C2) for the following reasons:

- **In C1 we operate from Holy Spirit life rather than soulish life (i.e. mind, will, emotions) in C2**. Choosing C1 results in a constancy of life, a balance that can deal with the troubles and successes of life without lurching continually from the mountain top to the valley. The latter tends to happen when we rely on our emotions and other components of our soul. The overarching principle here is that we are thankful to God for our amazing mind, will and emotions but they should first be subject to the Holy Spirit of God in our lives. Our mind, will and emotions will flourish and become a real asset in our lives when they are led and directed by the Holy Spirit of God.
- **In C1 we are a receiver NOT an achiever (C2) because we work and operate FROM and not FOR the Kingdom of God**. This means we become Christ-centred rather than self-centred, which saves us from being disappointed, feeling a failure and again being grumpy!!! It also deals with the spirit of religion, which is all about seeking performance to please God, rather than seeking the presence of God where we can approach His throne of grace and mercy, all the time, as loved sons and daughters. (Hebrews 4:16)
- **Dwelling in C1 leads to revelation rather than just information (C2).** Dwelling in C1 tells us again and again that we are our Heavenly Daddy's happy thought, every

second of every day. In the film called "Hook" based on the Peter Pan story, we see that Robin Williams (the adult Peter Pan) rediscovered his ability to fly when he found his happy thought; which was the birth of his first child, Jack. Dwelling in the revelation of God and what he thinks and knows to be true about us has the effect of releasing us to live according to our destiny rather than our history. We are not the sum of our experiences or the sum of information about us. This life principle and revelation means that we see other people around us according to their amazing destiny and potential rather than their history and their accompanying baggage. The latter can cause people to look back and lose sight of their purpose and calling.

- **The Kingdom of God alignment for the assignment flows from C1** whereas it is the other way around in C2. Assignments cannot drive the alignment we need for our Heavenly resources, strategy or blueprint. If we try, it usually results in burn out, being grumpy, disappointment and vows which sound like "I'll never try that again", "I'll always be a failure", "I never complete anything that I have started". It is important not to let our actions (assignment) define our purpose (alignment) and vision. This is particularly important if you are part of a leadership team responsible for shaping the vision, direction and actions of a body of people such as a company, church etc.
- **In C1 we are looking to see who we can bless** whereas in C2 we are always looking for "bless me". When we are in that place of rest and acceptance, our identity stems from that place of love, from Jesus who is the perfect expression of God's love. In addition, we naturally find ourselves in a place of abundance as one of the Hebrew names for God is 'El Shaddai'; this describes him as the all-sufficient one or 'He who is more than enough'. Occupying this position in life means that it becomes easy to pour out to others from that

overflow of abundance. As Psalm 23:1-3, 5 says in the Passion Translation:

The Lord is my best friend and my shepherd. I always have more than enough. He offers a resting place for me in his luxurious love. His tracks take me to an oasis of peace the quiet brook of bliss. That's where he restores and revives my life... you give me all I can drink of you until my heart overflows.

- **C1 is a place of habitation (in the love of God) and not just visitation**. You would never regularly say to your best friend that you only have time to call to see them at their house for few moments now and again at your convenience, then hurriedly leave halfway through your conversation and cup of tea or coffee. On the contrary, you would look forward to spending as much time as you can with your best friend over lunch. The time will fly by and the lunch may spontaneously extend into dinner and into the evening as you may lose all track of time. Your friend's house becomes a place of habitation and not simply passing through or visitation. How much more with the love of God, our greatest friend and supporter.
- **C1 is our place of rest where we are working FROM our inheritance as opposed to C2 where we are working FOR our inheritance.** In C1 we are operating as a son and daughter of the living God and our inheritance is guaranteed and will never perish, spoil or fade (Ephesians 1:14, 1 Peter 1:4). By contrast, in C2 we are working FOR our inheritance, in other words operating in the role of orphans (see Chapters 7 and 8), which is not the true relationship with God (Romans 8:15-16 and John 14:17-19) and which is often characterised by performance and drivenness.
- **In C1 it is who you are in Jesus Christ that compels you to do what you do**, whereas in C2 there is the lie that says "it is what you do that makes you who you are". Again, this comes down

to identity, namely that if we do not have the relationship and understanding of BEING a child of our Heavenly Dad (which Jesus modelled) then our identity stems from our DOING.

- **In C1 we receive the wisdom and security to discern which battles we are meant to fight.** Otherwise we find ourselves in C2 without any strategy, fighting all the battles and then we become worn out and defeated very easily. Great kings didn't fight every battle, they chose which were the crucial ones that would win the war. In addition, they didn't fight their battles in the same way each time. For example, King David chose different methods in battle according to the revelation of God, even to the point of advancing only when he heard the sound of marching (i.e. the Heavenly army) in the balsam trees (1 Chronicles 14:15, 2 Samuel 5:24).

This illustration using the two chairs is my workplace and marketplace modification and application of a message entitled the Three Chairs. This has been replicated by many preachers but is universally attributed to Pastor Leif Hetland as the original source. The third chair in his message relates to people who have not received Jesus as their saviour. Whether we have two or three chairs, the overriding principle is to ask the Holy Spirit of God to direct and spiritually glue us to Chair 1, in the place of rest. It is the best thing for us; in addition, it will wear out the enemy of our lives and his demons who really wants us out of Chair 1.

Choose a simple step today to accept and believe that you are your Heavenly Daddy's happy thought, and this will begin to help you place yourself in Chair 1. From there you will begin to follow God's lead, living from knowing that he sees you with the eyes of love based on your amazing destiny rather than your history. Let us discover more about this divine love story in the next two chapters from the place of Chair 1 as we also discover that a fruit of this story is that a dream can change a nation.

The next two chapters are quite a deep dive into the transforming ocean of God's love and my prayer is that you discover all the facets of these deep places. If you have not given your life to Jesus, I would encourage you to consider it now using the prayer in Chapter 10 so that you can squeeze the most out of these chapters. It will free you to explore below the surface and discover the life transforming treasures of your calling, destiny and purpose on Planet Earth.

Fiery heart

Chapter 7

THE DIVINE LOVE STORY
Part 1
Getting into Shape with our Heavenly Blueprint

- You Unravel Me with a Symphony of Love
- Following the Way of Love Helps Us to Process a Dream
- Your Heavenly Blueprint
- Get in Shape
- Keep in Shape

You Unravel Me with a Symphony of Love

It is often said that dreams are God's night parables of love as he sings over us with a Heavenly love symphony.

> *The Lord God will quiet you with his love and rejoice over you with singing.* (Zephaniah 3:17).

During the day, and also during the approximately one-third of our lives we spend asleep, the love overtures of Heaven are cascading over us. The Bible tells us in the Song of Songs 5:2 that "*while we sleep our heart is awake*" to hear these sounds of love knocking at the door of our heart. In fact, this represents a time when we are highly susceptible to receiving divine love as there is no resistance from our minds and the activities of the day whilst we sleep. We can freely "*experience the endless love of God cascading into our hearts through the Holy Spirit who lives in us*" (Romans 5:4-5 TPT). This scripture hints at a divine order which is unpacked further in Ephesians 3:16-19 where it is the Holy Spirit communing with our spirit in our inner being which allows our heart to encounter the amazing love of God. At this point our minds are then able to grasp the multi-dimensional love of God, as we read in the Passion translation of these verses:

> *And I pray that he would unveil within you the unlimited riches of his glory and favour until supernatural strength floods your innermost being with his divine might and explosive power. Then, by constantly using your faith, the life of Christ will be released deep inside you, and the resting place of his love will become the very source and root of your life. Then you will be empowered to discover what every holy one experiences – the great magnitude of the astonishing love of Christ in all its dimensions. How deeply intimate and far-reaching is his love! How enduring and inclusive it is! Endless love beyond measurement that transcends our understanding – this extravagant love pours into you until you are filled to overflowing with the fullness of God!*

This explosion of love by the Holy Spirit within our spirit is revealed to our hearts BEFORE our minds and not the other way around. This is important, and is seen again in Paul's second letter to the Corinthians:

> *For God, who said, "Let light shine out of darkness, made his light shine in our hearts to give us the light of the knowledge of God's glory displayed in the face of Christ. (2 Corinthians 4:6).*

In other words, the reality of God's light explodes into our hearts and it is this very event which provides the knowledge to inform our minds. This process is part of the transformation and renewing of our minds which is described in Romans 12-1-2. This supernatural reality makes a lot of sense if we think about how we fall in love in the natural world, where our minds often have to catch up with that first love exploding within our hearts. Our spiritual life suffers when we abandon our first love for Jesus (Revelation 2:4). An American friend from Maryland recently put it this way:

> I heard Papa God saying that He wants us to do an about-face. He desires us to turn and go back to the time when we first fell in love with Him. When we called Him our first love. The time when nothing else mattered but our precious time with Him. Our 100% back with Him. Waiting and listening for His whisper and delighting myself on His lap and leaning on His chest. No distractions and just my Daddy and me.

It comes back to the concept that we looked at in the previous chapter of "habitation in God's loving arms" rather than visitation. I would like to systematically go deeper into the benefits and outworking of resting in God's love. The process of rest provides an opportunity to restore, repair and recover. As a scientist working all over the world on skin beauty and ageing, it really does sound like a beauty treatment or regime doesn't it? We know from Queen Esther's story in the Bible that twelve months of beauty treatment (soaking in perfumes and oils) gave her access to a royal position from which she was then used to save a nation. That is a pretty good outworking of yielding to the restore and repair process.

In the worship song "No longer slaves" by Jonathan David and Melissa Helser, the opening lyrics are "You **unravel** me with a melody". We hear it a lot, but why is it necessary to be unraveled or undone by the love of God and how is it linked to this restore and repair process?

As a scientist, the beginnings of the answer to this can be seen in the natural realm when one considers the repair process for the replication of DNA in every cell of our body. Our DNA, our human genome, is arranged as a helix structure comprised of two facing DNA strands. For the DNA to be replicated, the two strands of DNA need to be separated or **unraveled** (by a family of enzymes knows as Helicases) into single strands. These single strands are now easily accessible to the repair enzymes that patrol up and down the DNA strands correcting and repairing any mistakes or blockages in advance of the process of replication. This is important as our cells do not want to replicate damaged DNA; this can cause disease and adversely influence the ageing process.

How much more in the supernatural realm, when one considers our spiritual DNA and how we are meant to spiritually replicate ourselves and also imitate the work of the Holy Spirit in the lives of others (Hebrews 6:12; 3 John 1:11). As Paul says in 1 Corinthians 4:16, *"Therefore I urge you to imitate me"*.

We can now imagine the supernatural rest and repair process where we are unraveled by the melody of divine love during the resting process thereby allowing the repair of our spiritual DNA. Some of the repairs will be linked to our identity, hurts of the past (relationships and situations) or bitterness in our lives; others may be linked to false loyalties and a false sense of duty. These all represent blockages in the spiritual DNA thereby preventing the DNA photocopier machinery from moving along and freely copying the DNA in the process of replication. Replication leads to multiplication which we know is an inherent biblical principle. For example, as God says to Abram, who became the father of the Israel nation (i.e. an amazing example of multiplication):

> *I will make you into a great nation, and I will bless you; I will make your name great, and you will be a blessing.* (Genesis12:2).

False loyalties will always hold us back from multiplying and being fruitful in the calling that God has for our lives. A false loyalty can take the form of holding on to something which was a commanded work of God but the season for that work has ended and you are still carrying on, even though the grace to do the work has lifted. False loyalties will always take you out of, or keep you from, your spiritual and physical sphere of influence where you are destined to have dominion and be fruitful (more on this later in the chapter).

How do you spot false responsibilities and false loyalties? Rebecca King (founder of Invictus Prophetic Network) describes how she knows this when she starts having dreams in which she has outgrown the bed (British Isles Council of Prophets 2020 broadcasts). This is interesting, as the symbol of a bed in dreams represents a place of rest. In my life, I have a similar dream in principle to Rebecca's, but it features the roots of a plant hitting the limitations of the pot in which it is planted, in other words it is time to be replanted to a bigger pot.

Allowing God to deal with false loyalties and responsibilities will allow us to be planted in the right place. It allows us to be part of our tribe, our spiritual family where we can be ourselves and be how we were made to be (according to our spiritual DNA). Being planted in the right place allows us to flourish and celebrate the pot we have been planted in. Otherwise, if we stick around in the small pot when we should have moved, then we can find ourselves complaining about the pot (this can represent our church, job etc.) and how we feel limited or trapped.

In this circumstance, it may not be the fault of the pot, it may simply be that the time to be re-planted has come. It is the time for you to yield to this and then do something about it. In this scenario, the issue may lie with you and not the pot. It is wise, therefore, to be re-planted once you feel your roots touching the edge of the plant pot and before you start becoming critical of the pot. Of course, decisions like this are important and should not be taken impulsively without finding confirmation from the guidance of the Holy Spirit and the loving will of the Heavenly Father.

We can see how bitterness, anger, stress of relationships, wrong actions etc. can affect our spiritual DNA. This may cause us to be resistant to being unraveled by the Heavenly symphony of love. Interestingly in this respect, there are some reports proposing that a similar scenario may possibly occur in the physical realm in human DNA. Dr Caroline Leaf describes work performed by McCraty and cell biologist colleagues (Leaf, 2013; McCraty, 2003) who reported that emotions can change the physical structure of human DNA. This provocative study reported that thinking and feeling anger, fear, and frustration apparently caused DNA to change shape according to these thoughts and feelings. The report details that DNA responded by tightening up and becoming shorter, thereby switching off many DNA codes. The authors conclude by proposing that the DNA is almost shut down by negative emotions.

They went on to report that the negative shutdown or poor quality of the DNA codes was reversed by feelings of love, joy, appreciation, and gratitude which caused the structure of the DNA to unravel and become 'relaxed' (which is a scientific term for the unwound conformation of DNA) thereby making the DNA codes more accessible to be switched back on. The authors of the report suggest that the DNA appears to be unraveled by positive emotions.

Clearly, as with any experimental observations, to be fully accepted in the scientific world it is standard procedure for findings to be verified by different groups in different laboratories and with a greater dataset of researchers. Therefore, there is clearly more work to be done to verify or disprove these provocative findings. Interestingly the broader conclusions from this study, however, are not contradictory to the general narrative of the widely published effects of positive feelings, meditation of love and so forth in the benefit of health. This includes phenomena such as the placebo effect and the positive effects of prayer. There is some interesting scientific evidence proposing that meditation linked to relaxation and cognitive wellness techniques can improve the quality of life of patients and the therapeutic efficacy of disease treatments in cancer, cardiovascular disease, psoriasis, chronic pain, depression and anxiety disorders (see Chapter 10, Gotink et al., 2015 for a summary).

Following the Way of Love Helps Us to Process a Dream

We can see the advantages of BEING unraveled in the love of God. Therefore, what about our DOING, namely our gifts and abilities (such as interpreting dreams) that we receive and use in that place of rest? Well, not surprisingly, the Bible tells us that our doing and gifting should flow from the place of being in the love of God.

> *Follow the way of love and eagerly desire gifts of the Spirit, especially prophecy.* (1 Corinthians 14:1).

Imagine a spy film, such as the Mission Impossible series, where the main character is spying on a suspect and following them, not letting them out of their sight. The spy then rings their support team to report the location of the suspect. At this point it is assumed that the location of the spy and the suspect are one and the same. In other words, you end up at the same place as that which you are following. Therefore, going back to 1 Corinthians 14 we see that if we follow the way of love then we end up being in the same place as love, namely BEING in love. We spend or sow our presence into where love is and so we are immersed, submerged in love so that we breathe love, hear love, see and touch love. As God is pure love, this abiding in love brings us in closer proximity to him who is love. This intimacy produces much fruitfulness in our lives including the revelation of Heaven which informs and helps our interpretation of dreams. In fact, in The Passion Translation Psalm 25:14 says:

> *There's a private place reserved for the lovers of God, where they sit near him and receive the revelation-secrets of his promises.*

We also read that when we are in the presence of Jesus, we find *"all the treasures of wisdom and knowledge"* (Colossians 2:3). Therefore, in the place of love and rest, lying close to God, we have access to revelation, secrets, wisdom and knowledge; this is where the **'revelation is given'** component of dream interpretation has its source. This helps us considerably when we must discern not only the source of the dream but how to process a dream. If the source, interpretation or application of the dream does not resonate with the symphony of God's love and rest around us then we would have to question bringing the dream and its consequences into our lives. This is an overarching broad or macro-scale principle, but let us see what this looks like on a micro-scale. First of all, here is a somewhat broad categorisation guide to identify the source of the dream. There are three possible sources, namely God and his Heavenly realm, the demonic realm or natural human aspects. Let us take the three in turn:

- It is important to note that the character aspects of the source are expressed in dreams. What do we mean by this? Well if the source is God who is love then one would expect the dream to exhibit characteristics from the heart of God such as love, peace, hope, destiny, creativity, strength, encouragement, comfort, guidance, instruction, freedom, liberty, cleansing, contending or warfare for yourself and others against evil or injustice. Dreams in this category are often in colour and events take place during the day.
- The source of the demonic realm is easy to identify as the expressed characteristics are the opposite of the Godly spiritual realm described above. They do not fit or resonate that place of rest, melody or symphony of love. For example, emotions such as fear, deception, anxiety, panic, feeling trapped, contained, hopeless, hate, dirty or unclean, aggressive to everything, are all representative of the demonic realm which ultimately wants to kill, steal and destroy (John 10:10). These characteristics are heightened in nightmares, in fact the word "nightmare" is derived from the Old English "mare", meaning a mythological demon or goblin who torments others with frightening dreams. The term has no connection with the word for "female horse". Dreams in this category are often in black and white and events usually take place during the night.
- Dreams caused by natural human aspects have been attributed to chemical and hormonal fluctuations, diet, or from our soul (i.e. mind, will and emotions) in origin.

Using this broad categorisation will help us to address the source of a large proportion of our dreams. However, the following micro-scale principles will test whether or not the God of Love in the Heavenly realms is speaking to us through our dreams. These are:

- Does the dream point to Jesus or God and lead you closer to him and the Heavenly values described above?
- Does the dream bring life and direct the dreamer to find and experience good fruit and for their life to flourish?
- Is the dream and its application consistent with the overall plan that God has revealed in the past for your life?
- Does the dream resonate or "ring true" with your spirit and is there an overall sense of peace?
- Does the dream encourage you to follow the way of love and peace?
- Does the dream promote unity and "oneness" (John 17:21-23) or does it produce disunity, arguments, divisions and factions?
- Does the dream align to and confirm the principles which are found in the written word of God?

The above process helps us with checking the revelation component of dreams. Once we have done this, we can proceed to interpreting the dream and then apply the outworking of its meaning in our daily lives. The process of Revelation, Interpretation and Application or R, I, A, is an important systematic tool for dream interpretation but also for other aspects of spiritual processing such as prophecy. A more complete explanation of this process can be found in my previous book (Birch-Machin, 2014, see Chapter 10).

Your Heavenly Blueprint

Dreams from God directly speak Heaven's purpose, calling and destiny into our lives, in other words, they are a Heavenly blueprint. This blueprint of who we are in Heaven is mirrored in our spiritual DNA as we manifest our Heavenly calling, destiny and purpose on planet earth. It is part of the *"let it be on earth as it is in Heaven"* principle that we read in the Lord's prayer (Matthew 6:10). As we go deeper into this we read:

> *All the days ordained for me were written in your book before one of them came to be.* (Psalm 139:16).

Therefore, the days of our purpose and destiny are written in a Heavenly book well before we ever took our physical place on earth. This is because Heaven is not limited by chronological time and is why Jesus can say to us that he is both the beginning (alpha) and the end (omega) in Revelation 22:13. There is a Heavenly blueprint which is the master document for our spiritual DNA. It influences us to be and to do what we were eternally made for on planet earth. Robert Henderson in his books on the courts of Heaven (Henderson, 2014, see Chapter 10) describes the importance of these Heavenly "Books of Destiny" in Psalm 139, as actual books or scrolls in Heaven that declare our purpose while on earth. If we look at the New King James translation of Psalm 139:16, King David (who wrote this Psalm) says of God:

> *Your eyes saw my substance, being yet unformed. And in your book they all were written the days fashioned for me.*

Here we have the connection between the Heavenly books and our spiritual DNA or substance. King David is describing that there is a book in Heaven that contains not only his makeup (spiritual DNA) or substance but also his destiny and purpose in life. What is more, God saw us functioning in the earth realm before it existed. Our books had their beginning through God *seeing* something before it existed, something that was yet unformed. God first saw it, declared it and then wrote our substance in our books of destiny and purpose. This substance or makeup is our spiritual DNA, namely what makes us spiritually unique and who we are as individuals.

In the miraculous way that the Holy Spirit influences our natural spirit (Ephesians 3:16) our spiritual and natural DNA may similarly be connected. This substance or spiritual DNA governs our gifts and abilities, what we are naturally good at versus what we find difficult. We can see from Psalm 139 that these things are linked to our calling and purpose as described in our Heavenly book of destiny. Therefore, when someone says, "I do not know what is in my book of destiny", a good first step in the answer is to direct the person to look at their gifts and abilities. These will be different for each individual, but they represent precious clues to what you were made for on planet earth.

What we were made for or simply put 'God's workmanship or artistry in our lives' is derived from the Greek term "poiema" meaning 'something that is made' or 'a work of art'. The Greek word itself is the word from which we derive *poem* in the English language. Therefore, we are God's poem as we allow him to fashion us. A poem has to be recited or read according to the original dictation rhythm in order to get the full effect intended by the author. When we step into our destiny, we discover a rhythm of the Spirit that we synchronise or get in step with. While Galatians 5:25 encourages us to *"keep in step with the Spirit"*, Matthew 11:28-30 shows what the "rhythm of the Spirit" looks like and how it is connected to the place of REST which I have previously described.

> *"Are you tired? Worn out? Burned out on religion? Come to me. Get away with me and you'll recover your life. I'll show you how to take a real rest. Walk with me and work with me – watch how I do it. Learn the unforced rhythms of grace. I won't lay anything heavy or ill-fitting on you. Keep company with me and you'll learn to live freely and lightly."* (Matthew 11:28-30 MSG)

These *"rhythms of grace"* are synchronized with the symphony of Heaven's love songs as we follow the way of love and are found in love. Remember it is the place of peace and rest where we are surrounded by the sound and rhythm of love that leads to the unravelling of our spiritual DNA, which in turn is connected to our books of destiny and purpose ordained for us. This rhythm of grace is connected to purpose as shown in the following scripture taken from 2 Timothy 1:9-10. In addition, it is found only in Jesus who through his death and resurrection connects us to his work of purpose and grace in our lives today.

> *He has saved us and called us to a holy life – not because of anything we have done but because of his own purpose and grace. This grace was given us in Christ Jesus before the beginning of time. but it has now been revealed through the appearing of our Saviour, Christ Jesus"* (2 Timothy 1:9-10).

We have seen that God works in us through his love, rest and the rhythm of grace to fashion our desires (linked to our spiritual DNA, our substance) to reflect what is written in our books of destiny and purpose, our Heavenly blueprint. Therefore, it follows that the unravelling or opening of our Heavenly books is a forerunner for that very same principle or process in our spiritual DNA. Indeed, we read in the book of the prophet Daniel that in the Heavenly courts of God the books were opened in the presence of the angels:

> *Thousands upon thousands attended God; ten thousand times ten thousand stood before him. The court was seated and the books were opened.* (Daniel 7:10).

It is encouraging to see that the angels get to look at what is written in our books. This will help them in their job description, which is to help and serve those who will inherit the salvation of Jesus (Hebrews 1:14). We are known, we are famous in the unseen realm. This must be part of the reason why the apostle Paul in the Bible encourages us to fix our eyes on what is unseen (2 Corinthians 4:18) and to listen to the roar of encouragement from the cloud of Heavenly witnesses (Hebrews 12:1).

This spiritual lifestyle approach is important as it counters the efforts of the demonic realm, which has an assignment to ensure that we feel unknown, insignificant and guilty as charged. This latter approach can introduce thoughts of wanting to quit and throw in the towel. However, we have an advocate (derived from the Greek word 'paraclete' meaning helper, adviser, counsellor) who completely counters this and speaks in our defence in the Heavenly realms, his name is Jesus (1 John 2:1).

We, therefore, have this amazing picture of the opening or unravelling of our books of destiny and purpose representing our Heavenly blueprint. This process is mirrored on earth as our substance or spiritual DNA (Psalm 139:16) is unravelled in the presence and rhythm of the divine love symphony. What does this Heaven on earth reality look like and how can we recognise it? This may be the subject of a booklet that I should write but for now here are few pointers:

- We know that the books of purpose are linked to grace and the place of rest. Here is a clue to what is written in our book or Heavenly scroll. For example, if we have the grace to do something, if it is easy and light to us (Matthew 11:28-30), then it is likely to be written in our book.
- According to the Heaven on earth principle of the Lord's prayer, the Heavenly blueprints in our books are now for us to activate on planet earth. In your profession this may look like an accelerated breakthrough process which would normally have taken much longer to be realised. Dreams are therefore important because your dreams are bridges that connect you with Heaven and the supernatural realm, particularly with these Heavenly blueprints.

A well-known example is the account of the discovery of the periodic table of elements that we learn about in chemistry class at school. The recognised father of the periodic table was the Russian chemist Dimitri Mendeleev. He was struggling to find an underlying principle that would organize the elements into sets of similar properties. It is recorded in his diary that after not sleeping for three days and nights he finally fell asleep exhausted and we read "*I saw in a dream a table where all the elements fell into place as required. Awakening, I immediately wrote it down on a piece of paper.*" Dream events, similar in principle, have happened in my own scientific research over the years.

On one occasion it resulted in a scientific breakthrough that was reported across the global press and media. The time between the blueprint revelation in my dream and the scientific breakthrough still took approximately two years, but without the supernatural blueprint I calculated that it would have taken orders of magnitude longer. This is an example from my world of science, you can simply apply the principle to your area of expertise or influence.

- Jesus is the only way to open or give access to the blueprints of Heaven written in our books or scrolls of purpose and destiny. He knows what is written in his scroll and he has the authority to open other scrolls (Revelation 5). It says in the book of Hebrews that Jesus said "*Here I am – it is written about me in the scroll*" thereby using the same words spoken prophetically generations earlier in Psalm 40:7. Jesus gives us another good example of knowing what is on his scroll, declaring it and being a fulfilment of a Heavenly blueprint. The account is found in Luke 4:17-21:

> *And the scroll of the prophet Isaiah was handed to him. Unrolling it, he found the place where it is written: 'The Spirit of the Lord is on me, because he has anointed me to proclaim good news to the poor. He has sent me to proclaim freedom for the prisoners and recovery of sight for the blind, to set the oppressed free, to proclaim the year of the Lord's favour.' Then he rolled up the scroll, gave it back to the attendant and sat down. The eyes of everyone in the synagogue were fastened on him. He began by saying to*

them, 'Today this scripture is fulfilled in your hearing'.

- The above point also answers the questions, how do you open the scroll, how do you read the book? Of course, like any church Sunday school quiz, the answer to this type of question is always Jesus. We read in Isaiah 29:11 that the seers and prophets could not access a Heavenly vision because it was like the "*words of a book (or scroll) were sealed*". Indeed, in the book of Revelation 5:1-2, we read that even angels proclaimed: "*with a loud voice, 'Who is worthy to open the book and to break its seals'.*" In the scenario described in the book of Revelation it was Jesus, depicted as the slain lamb, who was worthy to take and open the scroll.

  This also explains why prophets and seers are able to "read" destiny and purpose for both individuals and church congregations more easily during times of worshipping Jesus as he is the one who provides access. As a prophet, I know it is one thing to have words of knowledge about someone's past or present but there is a different anointing or sense of Heaven, when the future for that person is opened like a book. This is part of the "*calling things that are not as though they were*" described in Romans 4:17, a process that reflects both the fore and forth telling aspect of prophetic ministry.

  An example of this principle occurred when I was ministering at a church in the north east of England. It was not until I was worshipping in the church and focusing intentionally on Jesus that I became aware of a seven digit number with my spiritual eyes. The Holy Spirit instantly revealed the spiritual significance of these numbers that related to someone's calling and purpose. As I began to preach, I called out this number to see if it meant anything and a person responded saying it was their seven digit General Medical Council number which they used every day in their job as a hospital doctor. I then used this word of knowledge to call out the destiny, calling and purpose of that person in the resulting ministry time. What a privilege.

Get in Shape

Now back to the scientific analogy. Remember the process of spiritual DNA repair and restoration as we become unravelled in the love and rest of God? The purpose of this unravelling is to get us into the right shape so that we can multiply what God is doing in us when we are sent out into our sphere of influence. Indeed, the prophet Isaiah modelled this when he says *"I am undone"* or unravelled in the presence of God (Isaiah 6:5). This 'unravelling of Isaiah' was accomplished in advance of him becoming the right shape through the process of cleansing and restoration (burning coals) and then being sent out to his sphere of influence in those famous words *"Here am I send me"* (Isaiah 6:8). He was 'undone' before he was willing to be 'sent'.

As you know, I am a scientist and there is a living representation of the process exemplified by Isaiah, in the cells of our bodies every day. Let's have a quick science lesson. Many of the processes in our bodies involve proteins called enzymes which have a specific function, even now helping you to sit and read this book, in terms of our senses, our metabolism, breathing, movement and so on. Enzymes are called biological catalysts as they serve to speed up the rate of chemical reactions throughout our body. They do this by binding to substrates, the tighter or closer fit of the substrate with the enzyme, the faster the reaction rate. In other words, tight makes it right! This principle was originally described in biology as the lock and key theory. Even though this theory has been modified or replaced to accommodate other details, it provides a useful example to illustrate a principle for the purposes of this chapter. Specific enzymes bind to specific substrates to speed up a specific process which is crucial to keep our body working properly and healthy. If for some reason there is a change in the shape of the enzyme (for those who are interested, this is an area called the active site) then the substrate will not fit very well or tightly and the speed of the biological reaction will either slow down or stop which will adversely affect the workings and health of the body. A very small change in the shape of the enzyme – at the active site – can unfortunately cause severe and fatal illnesses. In other words, the shape of the key does not fit in the shape of lock very well.

Many scientific studies over many years (including those that I have been personally involved with) have shown that a major reason for the incorrect shape of the enzyme is due to accumulation of damage in that part of the DNA which is the template, or code, for making the enzyme. Therefore, the repair process of the DNA is important because it ensures the correct template exists to make the correct enzyme which has the right shape to tightly fit the substrate, leading to a rightly aligned and healthy body. It is like fitting two pieces of a jigsaw together, or as I have said earlier, a key into a lock. It is no good trying to force them together, every piece of jigsaw or key is a specific fit for its lock. In this biological jigsaw, the substrate is the partner for the enzyme, a perfect team. It is that alignment for the assignment principle we have already talked about in the previous chapter.

We can apply the above analogy to our spiritual DNA. This is simply where the repair and restore process, following the love-induced unravelling of our DNA, removes any damage or blockages. This allows our 'now restored' spiritual DNA to be an excellent template for making the right spiritual catalysts or enzymes which will in turn have the correct spiritual shape (lock) to fit the right spiritual substrates (key) leading to a thriving spiritual body. I like the word catalyst as it describes getting the correct things done very quickly as it speeds up a reaction. However, it is important to note that this process has its roots in the soaking and subsequent unravelling of our spiritual DNA in the love, rest and peace of God. So, when people come along and say things like "*what are you doing soaking in God's presence, it doesn't produce much*", then here is a worthwhile answer. It is not only spiritually true but also reflects the way that our bodies naturally work. If we want the Godly 'suddenlies' in our life, then we need to take the time to attend to our spiritual DNA which will lead to the catalysts in our life being exactly the right shape, speeding up all sorts of outcomes and fruit in our life. The keys will unlock our potential. This is so true, not only for the big decisions in life but also for those comparatively smaller but still very important Godly suddenlies that we need in our daily schedules.

For example, I regularly soak or rest in God's love as a daily routine on my own, but also at times with others, as I lead a lunch time soaking group called "Pit Stop". As the name suggests, the group serves to provide a place where people can make a stop for any running repairs or fine tuning of their lives during the working day. The session lasts for an hour and people are free to attend for as little as five to ten minutes or the full hour. The emphasis is more on celebrating the decision to sow our presence into the presence of God rather than a competition as to the amount of time which is committed. Many of the people who attend are from secular jobs in business or academia. The regular testimony at pitstop goes like this: Before they arrive, their mind is reminding them of the large 'to do' list of tasks and difficulties that need to be accomplished quickly and "what are you doing soaking when all this needs to be done, are you crazy?" After people return to work in the afternoon, not only do they feel more restored and repaired, some of the tasks and difficulties have already been mysteriously resolved and what would have normally taken hours to complete is usually accomplished in a fraction of the time. It is a testimony of suddenlies. I would even suggest that we particularly need to soak and rest in God's love at moments when we are feeling overwhelmed and do not feel that we have time.

In writing this I am reminded of an example showing the benefits of soaking to an everyday marketplace problem. I was encountering some seemingly insurmountable challenges around trying to employ several staff in my workplace team. Over many days, the more I tried to solve the problem the more I seemed to be going around in circles. Therefore, I decided to soak in God's presence on my office floor for 30 minutes during my lunch break and welcome God's access to the situation. Within a few moments after getting up off the floor, I received two e-mails telling me that not only had the situations been completely resolved but in addition I had been provided with a solution to another problem that I had not even asked God to solve. He gives us so much more than we can ask, think of or imagine (Ephesians 3:20).

Keep in Shape

Anyone who has gone on a diet or spent some time in the gym will tell you that it is important to GET IN SHAPE. However, they will also tell you that the next challenge is to KEEP IN SHAPE by maintaining all the benefit as part of our changed lifestyle. We know what this looks like in the natural realm but what about the choices and the lifestyle we need to adopt in the spiritual realm to KEEP IN SHAPE?

Clearly the obvious answer is described in the above, namely a lifestyle of allowing the love of God to work in our lives as this is the process that got us in shape. Let us go deeper into this and consider some of those characteristics which reflect being in the right shape and those that would threaten to distort or take us away from that shape.

1. Character and Gifting

This is an important issue to identify and address in order to keep in shape. In the spiritual DNA analogy described above, character is developed by submitting to God's repair and restore work in our spiritual DNA as we dwell in him. Character is developed in Chair 1 as described in the previous chapter and this helps us to realise that a gift is given but character is developed. Character provides the framework upon which the gifting can flourish but also be taken to places beyond what the gift is capable of alone.

For example, picture the branches of a tree that can grow and extend across a river bringing the gift of fruit to both banks of the river rather than just one side. Good character which is rooted in God's love will increase the reach of that gifting and enhance its influence. In times of hardship or times where the gifting is not abundant in a person's life then they are left with character. If their character is underdeveloped, then identity issues will likely manifest because that person's identity is tied to their gifting and not character. The example of hardship and suffering linked with character is seen in Romans 5:3-5:

> *we know that suffering produces perseverance; perseverance, character; and character, hope. And hope does not put us to shame, because God's love has been poured out into our hearts through the Holy Spirit, who has been given to us.*

What is worth noting in this scripture is that the fruit flowing from character is hope and hope is clearly rooted in soaking in God's love and this will ensure that we stay in shape. This principle is important, particularly if people are appointed to positions of leadership and responsibility as a result of their gifting rather than their character. When difficult and hard times are encountered in this situation, we often see that the person will find it difficult to operate from a great depth of character which in turn often leads to a lack of hope for the situation. We may observe the unfortunate scenario where people of great gifting but underdeveloped character "jump ship" when the situation becomes difficult.

The Romans 5:3-5 passage also shows us that character is linked to resilience or perseverance. A good example is the life of Joseph whose character was developed, through several very challenging events, to the point where he became the most influential and trusted person in Egypt after Pharaoh. An excellent way to encourage the development and fusion of character and gifting is through accountability to Godly leadership in the local Church. They will encourage you to fly high whilst safeguarding against pride and help you to see that your gift serves the Church instead of the Church serving you. King Uzziah was proud (described in 2 Chronicles 26:16) and consequently failed to listen to his priests and wise council. The result was that he became leprous and his reign was notable for the comparative lack of miracles.

In summary, it is character therefore and not gifting that will help us to keep in shape.

2. Orphan Spirit Versus the Spirit of Adoption

One easy way to find out whether you are operating in the orphan spirit or the spirit of adoption as a son or daughter of God is to see how you react to success in other people's lives. Do you celebrate their success and seek ways to encourage it even more in their lives (spirit of adoption) or do you resent it and bring it all back to yourself (orphan spirit) in a comparative and competitive manner. Or, try another scenario, how do you react to people when they tell you about some amazing spiritual encounter that you have not personally experienced but really wish could have happened to you? Do you pour out ridicule, put them and the experience down, cast fear on the whole situation (i.e. orphan) or do you celebrate and want to learn from that person (i.e. adoption)?

It is wonderful to read in the Bible that our adoption as children of God was always in his plan and brings the creator of the Universe great pleasure.

> *For it was always in his perfect plan to adopt us as his delightful children, through our union with Jesus, the Anointed One, so that his tremendous love that cascades over us would glorify his grace – for the same love he has for his Beloved One, Jesus, he has for us. And this unfolding plan brings him great pleasure!* (Ephesians 1:5-6, TPT).

We read in Romans 8:15 that it is not God's plan that we should be or feel like orphans because of the fact that he is our Abba, Papa, Daddy or beloved Father:

> *And you did not receive the "spirit of religious duty (slavery)," leading you back into the fear of never being good enough. But you have received the "Spirit of consecrated children (full acceptance/*

> *sonship)", enfolding you into the family of God. And you will never feel orphaned, for as he rises up within us, our spirits join him in saying the words of tender affection, "Beloved Father! (Abba)."* (Romans 8:15 TPT)

In the context of keeping in shape, being and behaving like an adopted son or daughter of God helps us to keep in shape whereas acting like an orphan causes us to begin to lose our shape. Using the terminology of Chair 1 and 2 described in the previous chapter, adoption is the place of rest (Chair 1) where we are working FROM our inheritance whereas in Chair 2 we are working FOR our inheritance as an orphan.

We have seen how to recognise when we are straying from operating in the spirit of adoption towards an orphan spirit in our reactions to other people's successes. Another key is how to identify and deal with the orphan spirit in others so that they do not drag you into their modus operandi. The first key is do not compete or match their orphan spirit statements as it will cause you to leave the place of love, acceptance and identity as a son or daughter. The second key is to use the correct vocabulary when a person is trying to manipulate and control you out of their orphan spirit.

Allow me to enlarge on this. Operating from your inheritance as an adopted child will always be a threat or offence to someone who is operating in the orphan sprit as they are working for their inheritance. This orphan derived tension is manifested as controlling actions in order to try and bring you out of your place of being into their place of doing and performance. This can become so strong that anything other than the word NO to the orphan spirit will be taken as a YES. For example in an attempt to placate or be nice (i.e. 'man-pleasing') you may say things like "OK, I will see…" or "maybe it will be possible".

To an orphan spirit this will be taken as a straight YES, a green light to start making their plans and organising their meetings in their way. Before you know it, you find out the next time you meet that things have already been put in place based on your 'maybe'. This causes you to begin to feel uncomfortable and trapped as things seem to have taken on a life of their own when really you meant NO on the inside. Sounds familiar? The kindest way to help the person with the orphan spirit in the long term is to give a clear NO. This will of course offend the orphan spirit, but it does give you the option to offer a Holy Spirit love motivated, wisdom alternative solution based on adoption. This will therefore build up the spirit of adoption in the relationship and not feed the orphan spirit.

3. Red Flag Statements

There are certain phrases or statements that are personal to us that we begin to use when our shape is beginning to become distorted. These statements are an early warning sign on our radar for us to realise that we are beginning to adopt the shape of orphan, based around striving and reliance on gifting only. Allow me to use a personal example of this principle in operation.

Many years ago I began to realise this principle in operation when I started to use phrases, particularly at my scientific work or at home, such as "who else is going to do that if I don't do it?" The result was that I was tempted to take on too much. I felt like I was being overwhelmed by the world and it was all on me to do it all "properly"! There are some key characteristics in the statements that may help you to identify the particular symptomatic statements in your life. First, it was a focussing on "self"; feeling that I had to do it all, to fix it and thereby leaving no room for God. Second, I was no longer in an exclusive place of being overwhelmed and unravelled by the love of God as my focus was being split by being overwhelmed by the tasks before me.

The key point here is where does our focus lie? It is true that we empower in our lives that which we focus on. Put it this way, whatever we look at and meditate upon becomes bigger in our lives at the expense of other things that become smaller and have less influence. Psalm 42 urges us to commune and focus on the right thing namely the overwhelming love of God:

> *as deep calls to deep in the roar of your waterfalls as your waves and breakers sweep over me"* (Psalm 42:7).

I would encourage you right now to prayerfully ask Jesus to show you those red flag statements that you make in your lives which are an early radar warning showing that you are getting out of shape. These are the shape distortion statements. Once you have identified them, then turn around, change direction and run back to that place of rest, adoption, love, character so that your shape can be restored and then be kept in shape. In addition, it is important in this process that you do not criticise and beat yourself up in the blame and condemnation game. This only serves to do the work of the demonic realm, for we know that there is no condemnation in Christ Jesus (Romans 8:1).

Chapter 8

THE DIVINE LOVE STORY
Part 2

How a Dream Can Change the Land

- Fit the Field
  - Giving our "Yes"
  - Resisting the Distortion of Your God Given Shape
- Benedict and Changing the Atmosphere
  - Power and Authority
  - Sound and the Land
  - The Time to Benedict
- Activation

Fit the Field

Now that we have covered GETTING IN SHAPE and KEEPING IN SHAPE, we can address its purpose or application. We are now the correct shape to FIT THE FIELD or sphere of influence that God has given us. Allow me to remind you of the spiritual DNA and catalyst analogy. Our restored and repaired spiritual DNA is an excellent template for the correct spiritual catalyst or enzyme (lock). This will, in turn, have the right spiritual shape to fit the correct spiritual substrates (key). The more complete or tighter the fit (i.e. the better the key fits in to the lock) then the greater the scope, acceleration and harmony of the activated spiritual processes, leading to a thriving and fruitful spiritual body. What are we meant to fit? Well, God has given us all a field or sphere of influence that we are designed to fit.

This is why it is important that we are the correct shape and keep the shape that we are designed to be in accordance with Psalm 139:16. The apostle Paul writes about this principle of our field in his letter to the Corinthian church:

> *We, however, will not boast beyond proper limits, but will confine our boasting to the field God has assigned to us, a field that reaches even to you.* (2 Corinthians 10:13).

In his book "Prophetic Company", Dan McCollam (Bethel Church, Redding, USA) defines the field that God has given us in this manner: "*Your gift works everywhere on everyone but works best somewhere on someone*". Paul Fenwick (Byker City Fellowship International, UK) defines the field of God as "*our sphere of influence where we are authorised to function, to have success, dominion and where we overcome*".

We can see these two definitions at work when we look at the actions of Jesus at the pool of Bethesda (John 5:1-14). He did not heal all of the great number of sick people who were there (verse 3). The account tells us that he just went to the one who had been there thirty-eight years trying to get in as the water was stirred. Jesus healed the man and then walked out of that place. There is no record of him following this up by going around and healing everybody else, in fact people at the pool asked the healed man "*Who is this fellow who told you to pick up your mat and walk?*" (v12).

In this instance, Jesus was not commissioned to go around and pray healing for everyone. This is because his field or sphere of influence and the linked manifestation of authority was simply to do that one thing. Jesus only did what he saw his Father doing (John 5:19) even though he also knew it is the will of the Father that all should be healed. In addition, Jesus had also been in situations where all who were ill were healed as he ministered to them (Matthew 8:16 and Matthew 12:15).

If we apply this principle to today, we have seen many occasions (probably involving ourselves) where Christians would pray for and see the healing for that one person to whom the Heavenly Father was directing them towards. Then, even though there was an absence of any further instructions from the Holy Spirit, they would spend the next few hours following up this amazing healing by praying for everyone they can find, but with the outcome that no-one else was healed. The result is that they would walk away quite dejected having only seen one healing out of many attempts, when the commission on that day was to pray for one person. If they had kept to the Holy Spirit plan, the "success rate" would have been 100%.

By contrast, in the other scenario the success rate would be much lower and the testimony may even serve to discourage rather than encourage, with take home messages such as "*you've got to pray for 100 people to see one healed*". This is not to discourage us from praying for many people on any occasion. It is simply meant to highlight that when we function in our sphere then we will be very successful and our testimonies will be full of what we are seeing rather than a focus on what is not happening.

Here is another example in the Bible. Take the story from Matthew 20:1-16, of the vineyard owner hiring workers to labour in his vineyard all the way up to the eleventh hour. To ensure that all the grapes were picked, the vineyard owner would not have let the workers wander around randomly in the vineyard or allowed all the workers to congregate in one area. Instead, he would have allocated specific areas to each worker, namely, their sphere or field. This strategy ensures that the whole of the vineyard is covered by all of the workers with the result that all the grapes are picked. This ensured that nothing was missed and the workers each received their reward. **This is the heart of our Heavenly Father, that no-one is missed or neglected as each of us works in the field that God has given us.**

In speaking about the field or sphere of influence that God had given to him, the apostle Paul continues in 2 Corinthians 10:15-16:

> *Neither do we go beyond our limits by boasting of work done by others. Our hope is that, as your faith continues to grow, our*

area of activity among you will greatly expand, so that we can preach the gospel in the regions beyond you. For we do not want to boast about work already done in another man's territory.

There are two principles to highlight in this scripture linking it with the story of the vineyard:

1. Keep to your assigned territory or sphere of influence.

This territory may be geographic, demographic or sociographic. We learn from this scripture that if we are to be effective, we must stay within the sphere that has been granted to us by God. The word in the Greek language for sphere is *'metron'*. It means a measure or limited portion. When we operate in this metron we have success and protection whereas outside of our metron we interfere and get in the way of other peoples' metron. This not only violates a culture of honour with our co-workers, but it leaves us open to demonic attack as we only have manifest authority or dominion to operate in our metron, our field.

This lesson was learnt the hard way by some Jews who tried to command evil spirits to come out of the seven sons of Sceva (Acts 19:13-17). The evil spirits answered, "*Paul I know about, but who are you?*" and the possessed man beat up the Jews. Therefore, be wary of following a formula rather than following the Holy Spirit's instructions that show you where your field or sphere of influence exists; operating in this field releases authority. Indeed, Psalm 16:6 says:

The boundary lines have fallen for me in pleasant places; surely I have a delightful inheritance.

If we keep to the confines of our field, then all will go well and we will complement the work of other workers in other neighboring fields. However, there is often the tendency to want to either work in another man's territory (against the advice of Paul in 2 Corinthians 10:16) or to try and move their boundary lines without permission (Deuteronomy 19:14) which can additionally result in a curse:

> *Cursed is anyone who moves their neighbor's boundary stone.* (Deuteronomy 27:17).

The demonic realm, the principalities and powers, described in Ephesians 6, know this principle very well which is why they will try absolutely anything to coax you out of your sphere of influence.

2. The need is not the call

In the description of the choosing of the seven in Acts 6, there was a large commotion amongst the growing number of disciples that certain people were not being fed. Here there was a need and consequently a choice for the twelve disciples to make. Should they continue in their God-given sphere of influence or should they neglect this and meet a need which was in the sphere of others? Peter summarized the decision which the disciples made in saying:

> *It would not be right for us to neglect the ministry of the word of God in order to wait on tables. Brothers and sisters, choose seven men from among you who are known to be full of the Spirit and wisdom. We will turn this responsibility over to them and will give our attention to prayer and the ministry of the word.* (Acts 6:2-4).

This is not a question of ability as the disciples could easily have met the need by serving food on the tables, it was a question of keeping to their sphere of influence. Their decision not only kept them ministering the word which sustained the spread of the word of God (Acts 6:7) but it released seven other disciples into their sphere of influence. This latter work by the seven disciples also facilitated in a natural way the increase in the number of disciples in Jerusalem.

This example highlights the fact that the need is not the call, it should not dictate what you should do and where you are to operate. This is clearly not an excuse to show a lack of compassion or hold back from being compelled by love. It is to ensure that we avoid having all the workers in one place, if we refer back to the workers in the vineyard example. (Matthew 20:1-16).

Allowing your mind, will and emotions (i.e. your soul) to be affected by need and circumstances will always pull you out of your sphere. In addition, it can put you into a 'Martha mode' as described in the Bible where "doing" is everything. In addition it can also prevent others from operating in their sphere because you keep getting in their way as they go about their work in their field.

Giving Our "YES".

A key principle in keeping to your sphere of influence is knowing what you have said YES to. The first part of this process is to look at the areas of your life and ask God which of these are your sphere and which are not. The second part is then to simply give your YES to those things which are in your sphere of influence. This will allow you to say no to those things outside your sphere including needs that are in someone else's field. Giving and knowing your YES has a number of benefits as follows:

a) It will prevent you from running someone else's race and ensure you will be successful as you act with the authority that comes from the commanded works in your field.
b) This principle also addresses burn out as it means that we only do what our Father God has assigned us to do.
c) Furthermore, God gives us the time to do that which he is asking us to do and not the time to do things which are not in our sphere of influence. If we grasp this principle in increasing measure, we will see our vocabulary change and we will stop saying things like "*I do not have time to do this and this*" and "*look at my diary I can't fit any more in*".

d) In this context, giving and knowing what our YES is to God as an increasing habit in our lifestyle really helps us to "*walk the talk*". It enables us to be more of a "completer" where our words match our actions and vice versa. Knowing what we have said YES to in the Heavenly realms helps us to discern what to say YES to in the earthy realm as there will be a "fit" with our field. The talk and the walk will be connected as there will be grace, favour and authority to enact that YES as a physical entity in our field.
e) You will find an empowerment as you will be operating in the commanded authority of your sphere of influence. Giving your YES to God automatically means that you shift and align yourself to pleasing God rather than man or a need based pleasing modality. This is important as it safeguards the shape we have become whilst in the place of rest and love of God.

This all means that first fueled with the love of God, we can then secondly address those needs in the designed, God-given, field in which we fit and where we can unreservedly pour out that love.

> *For it is Christ's love that fuels our passion and motivates us, because we are absolutely convinced that he has given his life for all of us. This means all died with him, so that those who live should no longer live self-absorbed lives but lives that are poured out for him – the one who died for us and now lives again.* (2 Corinthians 5:14-15 TPT).

Resisting the Distortion of Your God Given Shape.

Allowing ourselves to be influenced by needs, people pleasing, circumstances, relationships and groups which have no part in our destiny and calling will all serve to distort or stretch our God ordained shape (Psalm 139:16). Operating in your field which fits and reinforces your shape will create healthy boundaries. These will protect you from people making unauthorized withdrawals of your time, emotions and resources as you have not given your YES to that demand. In this regard, it will also help you to discern which of your relationships, connections and groups are healthy or are self-need based with roots in the orphan spirit.

Situations are need-based if people pursue you to be part of them so that they can make a withdrawal or take from you, either intentionally or unknowingly. In blunt terms, it is a form of asset stripping which is a term frequently used in the business world where the valuable parts of a company are taken without any regard for the future outcome of that company. This may be quite difficult to discern if, for example, you belong to a group or team run by need-based leader/s who are saying the right things; such as an emphasis on the good principles of connection, belonging or service.

There is a simple test to discern whether the motivation is need-based as there is often a facet of control involved. Control does not become manifest when you join a group but only when you try to leave. Need-based control will manifest when a temporary withdrawal or downscaling of your commitment to the group is communicated. This control is usually seen as (1) a disproportionate response typically involving an emotional overreaction (or other terms such as 'a melt-down' or 'throwing toys out of the pram') to your "distancing" and/or (2) telling you to stay and what you should do often accompanied by the misuse of words such as honour.

This scenario is universal, including the church, secular and business world. The need-based response in people has its roots in the orphan spirit and one of the fruits of this spirit is control. Control serves to pull you into its own perception of your shape which as a consequence will distort you from your God given shape. As the key does not now fit the lock so well, then you begin to find that unlocking fruit and potential becomes more difficult which can breedfrustration.

Here are some descriptions of how to recognise control and need based attempts at distorting your God given shape.

The most obvious manifestation of control on your shape is where you feel compressed or contained. There is a sense of "there is no way out", of being trapped, there is a lack of freedom and you may find yourself saying "I have no option".

The more subtle expressions of control serve to distort your shape rather than contain it. Distorting your shape will mean that your shape will be stretched so that you do not so easily fit your field or sphere of influence, thereby reducing your daily effectiveness in your sphere. Your shape can be distorted in two ways, by being pulled forwards or backwards:

Distortion Backwards – False loyalties, responsibilities and a false sense of duty will all serve to pull your shape back to what it used to be like before you allowed the love of God to get you into shape for your new sphere of influence. This type of shape distorter can take the form of the old ways of doing things for which the season has already passed. The book of Isaiah and the letter to the Philippians put it this way:

> *Forget the former things; do not dwell on the past. See, I am doing a new thing!* (Isaiah 43:18-19).

> *But one thing I do: Forgetting what is behind and straining toward what is ahead, I press on toward the goal to win the prize for which God has called me Heavenward in Christ Jesus.* (Philippians 3:13-14).

It can be a linking back to past relationships or environments which do not fit you anymore. There is therefore pressure to "fit in" with the old way in a people pleasing way. If you "fit in" with the old way, then you cannot fit your field in the new way. Remember it is far better to be an amateur in the new rather than an expert in the old, which is no longer relevant or has a purpose.

Distortion Forwards – Pulling your shape forward will also distort. This is seen as incorrectly accelerating things so that they occur prematurely and under developed; think about the example of a premature birth. This type of shape distortion comes in the form of hurried pressure. It may even be the pressure to do the right thing but at the wrong time. It is therefore important to pay attention to the people you allow (if any) in the delivery room when God is unravelling you with his love and changing your shape. There is an entire book that could be written about this.

If these shape distorters do not succeed, then need-based control will try another tactic which is to try and self-project elements of itself on to you. In people who are operating from need-based control, this can take the form of projecting their thoughts or attitudes on to you so that you can also adopt and wear them. This is akin to walking around in someone else's armour; something which the future King David found was completely useless when the current King of Israel (Saul) offered his armour to fight the giant Goliath (1 Samuel 17).

This **self-projection scenario** often happens when someone is not coping with a profound change in their life which they cannot control (such as the Covid-19 pandemic at the time of writing this book) but sees that you are thriving under the same circumstances. The reason you are thriving is that you have allowed your spiritual shape to be changed by the love of God so that you now fit the changing field or sphere of influence.

Self-projection from a need-based orphan spirit has the intent to try and cause you to revert to your old self and shape with its corresponding thoughts, attitudes and words. The orphan spirit part is evidenced in the fact that the person will feel better about not coping in their present circumstances if they can persuade you to join them in that scenario by accepting the consequences of their self-projection. Often people are not aware that they are doing this, it is usually unintentional but somehow, they "just can't help it". Whatever the reason, it is important to resist the shape distortion.

By accepting self-projection of someone who is operating in need based control, you accept the shape distortion which that projection can cause. Because of this you now begin to fit the old and therefore begin to struggle, having abandoned your new shape which was flourishing. In other words, there is the danger of you accepting their projection of your blueprint of destiny (usually to feed their own need) rather than flourishing in your Heavenly blueprint that is fashioned from the love songs of God. In both the work place and church I often observe self-projection from a need based orphan spirit which manifests in statements such as 'you were made/born/created to do this or that (you can fill in the gaps)' when your calling and shape clearly shows that you are designed and created for something completely different. The solution here is to resist the shape distortion from need based control and listen to the God who made you and is in loving care of your shape which fits your sphere of influence and destiny.

Information Feeds Control

Control will flourish when it can predict a response in you. This requires a type of deep level of information from you that reveals your dreams, desires, hopes, aspirations, strengths, weaknesses. Once you have divulged this deep personal information to control, then it has the means to predict your actions and thoughts and thereby exert its influence on your spiritual shape.

Clearly this is not a reason to disengage with deep God-given relationships and friendships with people. I have many of these and I treasure them, but it is always worth asking the Holy Spirit for discernment, particularly when someone is asking you to reveal deep personal information within the first minutes of talking to you (excluding counselling situations etc..).

Clearly this issue here is about who and what are we connected to. Connection for connection's sake can result in unwise and unhealthy relationships. If we first of all are connected with the Father heart of God in that place of love, security and rest, then the choice of who and what to connect with can be easily tested. For example, the potential new connection will either reinforce or take you away from that place of rest and peace. Therefore, following the way of peace is a good yard stick or plumb line here. As the prophet Jeremiah says:

> *ask where the good way is, and walk in it, and you will find rest for your souls.* (Jeremiah 6:16).

If we allow our shape to be distorted, then it attracts the wrong kind of things that will only serve to reinforce that shape, almost like a vicious cycle. On the victory side of things; if we resist the distortion of our God given shape then we attract those elements which will reinforce our new shape and ensure a much better outcome!-

In summary, allowing God rather than need to define our shape means that we are resourced by God to fit and flourish in our sphere of influence. The outcome of this alignment is that we can meet those particular needs which are part of our assignment. In other words, SHAPE comes first and then meeting the NEED that is in your field comes second. Of course, we clearly want to help people to flourish in life.

The key to this is staying in shape and remaining in your sphere of influence fueled by the love of God which allows you to tend your field (people, businesses, situations etc..) really well with great wisdom and knowledge (Colossians 2:3).

Benedict and Changing the Atmosphere Power and Authority.

Being unraveled in that place of rest, intimacy and love of God (see Chapter 7) means that the tune or sound in our heads for the day is not the latest track on the radio but it is the very heartbeat of God, the love symphony and rhythm of Heaven (Zephaniah 3:17). Power in the Greek is the word *'dunamis'* from which we get the word dynamite; it is the same word for the power that came on the disciples at Pentecost in Acts 2. Authority on the other hand is a completely different word in the Greek, it is *'exousia'* which means the power of rule of government that can command submission (dominion). Although authority is at times translated as power in some versions of the Bible, we see both terms are used in Luke 4:36 which says of Jesus:

> *With* ***authority*** *and* **power** *he gives orders to impure spirits and they come out. (emphasis added).*

Power from God is a gift delivered using his Holy Spirit, we do not do anything to deserve it when it comes. It is the manifestation of God's love for us that suddenly appears from the invisible realm into the visible realm. Exousia is something that you carry, it is not fleeting, it is a governmental entitlement, the highest authority possible that can exert rule of law and dominance (dominion) that is manifest in the invisible and visible realm (Matthew 28). Exousia will therefore always trump power, as shown for example in Mark 4 where the power of the winds was calmed and obeyed the authority in Jesus. In the historical culture of the Bible we read that kings conquered through power but ruled through authority, which was often symbolised through the holding of a sceptre. King Jesus clearly had both as seen in the Luke 4 passage above.

What is more, we walk in that same power and authority as we have this inheritance as sons and daughters of the living God. Psalm 23:4 reads "*your rod and your staff, they comfort me*", which is a picture of both provision of power and authority to us. The authority flows from our intimacy with the Lord as we lie down in his green pastures and quiet waters of rest and love (Psalm 23:2). The rod in Psalm 23 is the picture of power, it is what a shepherd typically used to beat off those animals such as wolves, bears and lions that would threaten the flock.

Just as a side comment here, this is a wonderful picture of those pastoral qualities which are willing to fight the equivalent of wild animals to protect their flock as opposed to running away at the first sign of danger. The staff in Psalm 23 represents authority, it is what the shepherd used to lean on and steady his walk. As we translate this spiritual reality to our sphere of influence, we see that God bestows us with both authority and power as we shepherd that field.

Sound and the Land.

God is waiting for us to step into all that he has created us to be (Psalm 139:16). Even the ground under our feet in our field or sphere of influence is groaning for us to exercise our exousia authority on earth as we take our place as children of God. This spiritual reality is described in:

> *For the creation waits in eager expectation for the children of God to be revealed.* (Romans 8:19).

> *We know that the whole creation has been groaning as in the pains of childbirth right up to the present time.* (Romans 8:22).

This authority, which can affect the land and the atmosphere around us in our sphere of influence, represents part of our inheritance as children of God and this inheritance can only come through a relationship with Jesus.

This principle takes us back to the starting place of rest and God's love where, as adopted children of God, our substance or spiritual DNA is repaired and restored. This results in a change of our spiritual shape so that we become a close fit for the field which God has given us, as we walk in the destiny ordained for us in the Heavenly books of purpose and calling of Psalm 139. In addition, it is this place of rest in which our heart is awake at night and where we are receptive to the connection with Heaven in our dreams. From the intimate place with God we speak out what we see and hear in the Heavenly realm. This very action will change the spiritual atmosphere around us on earth. Indeed, modern day physics has proposed that words and sound coming from our mouths are able to change or affect the physical environment or molecules around us.

The 'words are energy and energy affects matter' principle is described very succinctly by Steve Abley in his book, *The Return of the Musical Prophet* (2014). In this and other books on the subject, an example is given where God spoke the words "*let there be light*", and then the substance of light was there (Genesis 1:3). They suggest that the sound vibration of God's words caused the substance of light to manifest and become visible.

As we become our new spiritual shape fashioned by the love song of Heaven unraveling our spiritual DNA, then it is no surprise that our spiritual sound also changes. Imagine a musical instrument which relies on breath or a supply of rushing air going through it to create a sound. Any change of shape, either exterior or interior, or any extra holes in the instrument, will inevitably alter the sound which is emitted from the instrument. Given that this is true in the physical realm, then how much more in the spirit realm where we are that instrument for the Heavenly sound. The shofar is a good example of a physical and spiritual connection. In the physical, it is a ram's horn trumpet used in the Bible for battle (and now used in many Jewish ceremonies). In the same context of battle, we see that God sounds a ram's horn in the Heavenly realm:

> *The Sovereign Lord will sound the ram's horn and attack like a whirlwind* (Zechariah 9:14 NLT).

The ram's horn (shofar) in the Bible is also translated as trumpet and there is clearly a connection between the sound of the ram's horn (trumpet) and victory. Further examples include: (1) the fall of the walls of Jericho at the sound of the trumpet blast; and (2) the victory by Gideon against overwhelming odds. Gideon and his 300 men conquered the 135,000 Midianite soldiers armed with a ram's horn (trumpet, shofar) and a clay jar with a torch hidden inside. The sound of the ram's horn caused chaos in the Midianite camp and achieved victory for the people of Israel and the land that was occupied by the Midianites.

In the same principle, as we allow the breath (ruach) of God to blow through us by his Holy Spirit it will release a sound that is specific to the instrument shape that we have become. We will see freedom and liberation for the land and the people of that land as we begin to synchronise with the sound of the land or field that God has given us. This is why it is important to yield to the love symphony of Heaven which changes our shape so that we become the metaphorical shofar of freedom that the land is groaning for in Romans 8:22. This is another reason for resisting the distortion of our shape as it will change our sound which will adversely affect its synchronicity with that of the land.

Interestingly in the example of Gideon, the word Midianites means 'strife' or 'conflict' and so if you want to see strife removed from your community and land then I urge you to become the shape that will release the victory sound. Interestingly, Gideon's victory was sparked by a dream of a barley loaf (Gideon) rolling into the Midianite camp. This is a prophetic metaphor for the 'bread of life' (Jesus in John 6:35) rolling into the camp of our lives and community to remove the strife. In other words, the bread of life removes the strife!

There is also a spiritual legality in our words, particularly when it is in the form of declarations. This spiritual principle is connected to the authority that we have as children of God in the courts of Heaven as God takes his seat and the books of calling, purpose and declaration are opened (Daniel 7:9-10). On another occasion I would like to take a deep dive into this topic, but for now please refer to the excellent teaching by Robert Henderson and Ronald Montijn (see Chapter 10).

In summary, we see there is a connection between Heaven and the land upon which we walk. The land is affected by the declarations that we speak which are rooted in Heaven and in the scrolls and books which form part of our Heavenly blueprint. This is communicated to us in that place of rest and love through prayer, our dreams and by reading the word of God. The prophet Jeremiah demonstrated this when he said:

> *O land, land, land, hear the word of the Lord!* (Jeremiah 22:27-30).

It is not only the land which can respond to the life-giving words of Heaven, we see that circumstances, situations, destinies of people and cities can respond to these words of life. The metaphor for this principle can be seen in the Bible when the prophet Ezekiel spoke life to a bunch of dry bones which caused them to come alive:

> *Then he said to me, "Prophesy to these bones and say to them, 'Dry bones, hear the word of the Lord! This is what the Sovereign Lord says to these bones: I will make breath enter you, and you will come to life. I will attach tendons to you and make flesh come upon you and cover you with skin; I will put breath in you, and you will come to life. Then you will know that I am the Lord.'"* (Ezekiel 37:4-6).

The Time to Benedict

We see in the Jeremiah and Ezekiel passages from the Bible that there is great power in the speaking of blessing or wellness over the land, over dry or dead situations, relationships, cities, nations and so on. We are commanded therefore to speak well. The Latin word for this activity is to **BENEDICT,** which is where we get the word benediction. 'Bene' means well and 'Dict' means speak. There is a mandate or Heavenly blueprint to walk the land God has given you and to BENEDICT with Heavenly words of life in order to revive, restore and redeem it. This land may be represented as previous places of revival (spiritual, cultural, commercial) and situations that society and even the Church may have given up on (i.e. the Ezekiel dry bones).

These life-giving words are received in that place of rest and God's love, through prayer, the Heaven inspired word of God or even God communicating to you in a dream. As well as the individual authority and mandate to walk the land God has given you and to benedict Heavenly declarations to change the atmosphere, there is also a collective mandate for the people of God. There is a synergistic effect (i.e. where the sum of the whole is greater than the simple sum of the individual parts) when the people of God come together as the Ecclesia, a term describing God's legislative body, authorised to operate within the court system of Heaven.

This is a perfect time in history to BENEDICT over the land, people and situations. It is because from September 30th 2019 we have entered the decade of the 80s in the Jewish calendar as we have progressed from the year 5379 to 5380. In the Jewish alphabet the word which has the numerical value of 80 is the word 'Pey' (also called peh or pei). Pey is the 17th letter of the Hebrew alphabet and it means "Mouth". Therefore, the decade of the 80s is one where BENEDICTION, the use of the mouth to declare blessing, has and will have a special importance and significance. This will happen as we walk into all that God has promised us in our field according to our Heavenly books, as we abide in God's love and receive his love songs into our hearts through our dreams. The timing significance of 80 is underlined when we see that Moses was 80 years old when he led the Israelites out of slavery in Egypt as described in Exodus 7:7. This is also described in Deuteronomy 34:7 where we read that Moses was 120 years old when he died having spent 40 years wandering in the wilderness after escaping from Pharaoh and Egypt (120 minus 40 is of course 80 years old).

Moses saw the promised land, but he did not taste the fruits of the land; it was left to Joshua to cross the river Jordan and walk in that promise as his feet touched the land. This example of Moses seeing and Joshua tasting the fruits of the promised land, illustrates the second application of the meaning of Pey or the mouth. The first application is declaration from the mouth, namely benediction while the second application of the mouth is to taste and eat. The following scripture in Psalm 81:10 highlights this:

> *I am the Lord your God who bought you out of Egypt, open wide your mouth and I will fill it.*

There are two additional points of significance which link the 'Moses seeing and Joshua tasting' principle with the current transition of the Jewish calendar from the 70s decade to that of the 80s. The first point of significance is the connection shown in this verse:

> *Taste (Joshua) and see (Moses) that the Lord is good.* (Psalm 34:8 emphasis added).

The second point of significance is that, in the Jewish alphabet, the word which has the numerical value of 70 is ayin which represents "eye" and refers to physical as well as spiritual sight. Therefore, the progression from the 70s (eye) to the 80s in the Jewish calendar mirrors the progression of Moses seeing (eye) the land but Joshua tasting the land (mouth) in Psalm 34 and Psalm 81. Here we have a demonstration of the principle where something is seen and then it becomes manifest so that it can be tasted. This principle is continued in Romans 4:17 that God:

> *calls things that are not as though they were.*

In the Passion Translation it is expressed more simply as:

> *call into being things that don't even exist yet.*

The act of benediction and speaking out the words of life to the land and to the "dry bones" is a prophetic activation which has the ingredients both of forth-telling (i.e. causing the future) and the spiritual 'law of attraction' (as described by Patricia King, 2015). These are both encompassed in the Romans 4:17 scripture. This scripture describes the process that as we align to and benedict declarations of Heaven that are ordained in our books of purpose, then we attract or call into the here and now those very things which are promised in the books. We can therefore have our cake and eat it! Not only can we 'see' the promises like the example of Moses but that we can also 'taste' them like Joshua as we forthtell or call them into the here and now.

This Heavenly kingdom principle is clearly eternal, continuous and ongoing as Heaven's activities are independent of the time that we are living in. However, it is has been highlighted to us in this season of the decade of the current Jewish calendar which underlines the benediction and tasting of that which we have seen. The forthtelling prophetic principle in Romans 4:17 is accelerated by the operation of the law of attraction where we see the following dynamic at work in this scripture:

> *You will also declare a thing, and it will be established for you; so light will shine on your ways.* (Job 22:28 NKJV).

The spiritual law of attraction in this scripture reflects the spiritual reality of the magnetic effect of the spoken word which attracts or accelerates the connection with the ordained promises of the Heavenly realm to see it manifest in the earthly realm. This is connected to the principle that the life-giving word of God spoken from our mouths (as in a declaration or benediction) will change the atmosphere. We read about this principle in Isaiah 55:11:

> *so is my word that goes out from my mouth: It will not return to me empty but will accomplish what I desire and achieve the purpose for which I sent it.*

These principles in the Books of Job, Isaiah and Romans mirror the biological situation in our own bodies which I described earlier in the book. Allow me to recap, the catalyst or enzyme needs to be the correct shape to fit the substrate in order to accelerate the biological process for sustaining normal function and life in our bodies. If the catalyst is the correct shape then the biological law of attraction (Job 22:28) works strongly to pull or call the substrate from wherever it is in the cell to be (Romans 4:17) in close proximity to the catalyst. The binding of the substrate and the catalyst will accelerate a process so that a function in the body can be accomplished (Isaiah 55:11). This is so exciting; that the natural realm of our bodies reflects a Heavenly spiritual reality.

Let us go one step deeper in terms of considering these principles and how our atmosphere is changed as we speak, declare or benedict over the land that God gives us. As we allow ourselves to become the right shape and declare the "attractive" words of God then we begin to fit not only the land but the sound of the land. We read earlier that the spoken word of God fits the land (Jeremiah 22:27-30) and also the land makes a sound in eager anticipation of its redemption (Romans 8:19 and 22) and freedom. This includes the results of violation and conflict as Jeremiah 50:22 tells us that the noise of battle remains in the land. It is therefore not surprising to read in the Bible that if people tried to settle in the land without *"cleaning it up"* both physically and spiritually then it would *"vomit out its inhabitants"* as we read in Leviticus 18:25 and 28, and here in Leviticus 20:22:

> *Keep all my decrees and laws and follow them, so that the land where I am bringing you to live may not vomit you out*

We may therefore find it hard to operate in our particular geographical space or land space for two reasons:

- The land is not part of our field or sphere of influence or;
- The land has been contaminated, violated or polluted by previous or current occupants in some manner and requires freedom.

If we know that the land is part of our God given sphere of influence, then we can focus on the cleaning up process. The love symphony of sound in Heaven resonating over us (Zephaniah 3:17) changes our shape and sound to fit the field as we benedict over the land which then attracts into the present the purpose, destiny and restoration of the land which has always been promised (Romans 4:17). It is as though we become the tuning fork of Heaven's symphony of love which resonates with the sound of the land that is yearning to be restored to its original Heavenly design or blueprint. This is the reason why we have a sense of belonging or "right fit" when we walk into a place or city or nation. It is because (whether or not we perceive it) we are citizens of Heaven (Philippians 3:20) and as such we are designed to know the sound of Heaven and to fit or synchronise with Heaven.

As we see the land being freed and changed with our benediction and sound then we also see the benefits to the societal mountains of media, government, education, economy, family, religion, and arts and entertainment in our communities and cities and nations. What about the land which is represented by our own physical bodies, our mind, will and emotions? Well, in a similar fashion, the redemptive and healing sound of the symphony of love from Heaven declared from our mouths resonates in every cell, joint, marrow, thought, and attitude within our body and soul according to the principle in Hebrews 4:12.

In summary, this book not only takes us through how to prepare, receive and interpret dreams by skill and revelation, it shows us how a dream can connect us to Heaven, to the God of love. The amazing news is that the access, gateway or portal, has already been purchased for us by the sacrificial blood of Jesus. This book shows us how this amazing love, and the sound and symphony of that love, transforms us so that we can transform the atmosphere in our sphere of influence.

The beginning and the end of the chain reaction of love flowing from God in the Heavenly realms shows how a dream can transform the very land, a nation. The chain reaction or cycle of divine love is summarised below in bullet points. It is far better to be continually cycling through it rather than a one-off experience; so when you get to the end of the list below come back to the top and cycle through it again to engage in another breakthrough.

- Our very substance, our spiritual DNA is seen and ordained by our loving Heavenly Father in the Heavenly realms. Here, our Heavenly blueprint, the books or scrolls of calling, destiny and purpose are found.
- Here, there are the love songs of God singing over us.
- As we dream, our heart is awake to this symphony of love songs.
- As we allow the love songs of God to unravel our very substance or spiritual DNA, during the night and day, we enter into God's place of rest, repair and restoration.
- This is mirrored in our physical DNA which is unravelled so that it can be repaired and restored before it is replicated.
- Jesus, the expression of God's love, unravels our Heavenly blueprints or scrolls of calling, destiny and purpose. This love song and the rhythms of grace change our spiritual shape so that we begin to fit our sphere of influence more completely as written in our Heavenly blueprints.
- This process is mirrored in our natural bodies by a catalyst or enzyme fitting its substrate causing an acceleration of natural processes (a type of lock and key).
- Once we are in the correct "spiritual shape", there is the need to adopt a lifestyle of always being found in the love of God so that we keep in shape to fit the field or sphere of influence. This lifestyle will fit us like a glove, it will be tailor-made for us.
- Keeping in shape involves the dynamic of character vs gifting, spirit of adoption vs orphan spirit and resisting the distortion of our new correct spiritual shape.
- As we keep our shape, we fit the field, we keep to the boundaries of our field and we see increased manifestation of our authority.

- We benedict more effectively over the land and change the atmosphere as we become the instrument that speaks and resonates the love sounds of Heaven by which we have been unravelled. We are the shofar sound of freedom as God's breath resonates through us. We are also God's poem of love as we benedict over the land with the sounds and words of our Heavenly blueprint.
- By the principles of forthtelling and law of attraction this benediction of love calls into being those things that don't yet exist, but yet are written in the Heavenly books of calling, purpose and destiny.
- And so, we find ourselves back at the beginning of the love chain reaction of our blueprint in Heaven. By repeating this cycle as part of every detail in our daily lifestyle we will increasingly see more of our Heavenly blueprints becoming more visible in our physical realm as the Heaven on earth principle becomes an everyday reality.

This principle defined above is perhaps, as Dr Martin Luther King found out, why a dream can really change a nation and the world. GO DREAM!

Activation

As we draw this chapter to a close and before you go on to the next chapter, I would encourage us all to activate this love story even more in our daily lives or perhaps for the first time. The love symphony of God in Heaven unravels the very substance of our lives, our very spiritual DNA, to repair and restore so that we become the right shape to fit the field of purpose, our sphere of influence. It begins with following the way of love and finding yourself in that place of love and rest. It is expressed as a fruitful flourishing life that overflows with blessings for all those around you. The access to all of this is Jesus, who is the ultimate expression of God's love.

I often find it easier to remember and activate a process in my own life if I can summarise it to five key points which is not only the number of grace, but it maps very nicely to the number of fingers found on one hand.

So here we go, let's summarise the chain reaction or cycle of divine love to five points:

1. You have a **Heavenly Blueprint** which will become a physical reality,
2. God's love symphony unravels you to **Get in Shape,**
3. Abiding in his love song will **Keep you in Shape** to,
4. **Fit the Field** or sphere of influence,
5. **Benedict** to change the atmosphere, land and nation and see your blueprint become a physical reality.

Let us not delay any of this, the time is now for us all today to step further, higher and deeper. Do not allow external influences to put you off or delay this today. We read:

> *Whoever watches the wind will not plant; whoever looks at the clouds will not reap.* (Ecclesiastes 11:4).

True, there are some things that you cannot be sure of but if you wait for the perfect weather then you will never sow or reap. The Message Translation puts this verse quite bluntly:

> *Don't sit there watching the wind. Don't stare at the clouds. Get on with your life.*

Activation 1

Therefore, I encourage you to get on your own, turn your phone on to flight mode so you cannot receive calls, social media and e-mails but you can voice record what God will show you and your reactions to this. Now find that place of rest and love as you follow and tune in to the love songs of Heaven, the rhythm of his grace. You know the sound, yes you do! You were designed to fit into Heaven as you are a citizen of Heaven. Heaven fits you like a glove, it is on your spiritual passport (Philippians 3:20). As you gaze upon the beauty of God (Psalm 27:4), ask him three questions and then do the action described in the fourth point:

1. What does he think of you?
2. What does he want to say to you?
3. What (if anything) would he like you to do?
4. Now, from this place, practice seeing with the eyes of Jesus, such as seeing the gold and not the dirt. For example, Jesus called out Peter 'the rock' and not his other name, Simon which means broken reed. Think of a person in your life with whom you have the most problems, conflict, irritancy or simply intimidation. Ask God to reveal at least one aspect of gold in that person's life. Then seek for an opportunity to tell the person about how you value that nugget of gold in their life. As an experiment, observe how this positively affects and transforms your relationship with that person but also how that person begins to change how they interact with others.

   The benefit of this cause and effect activation will result in you seeking to do this more as your expectation grows each time. It will continue to grow until you do not have to be intentional about this anymore as it becomes part of your lifestyle, where you cannot help but see the gold. You will see the opportunity, the purpose and the way to release the calling and destiny in others!!

This fourth points highlights an important principle, namely that as we take the first step (in this case deciding to be in the place of rest and asking God to show us the gold) then we begin to see more clearly on every level of our lives. This principle is highlighted in the story of the healing of the blind man in the pool of Siloam. Jesus said to the man:

> *"Go," he told him, "wash in the Pool of Siloam". So, the man went and washed, and came home seeing.* (John 9:7).

In this account, the blind man was not healed until he washed in the pool of Siloam. Siloam means "sent", in other words this activation step made by the blind man resulted in complete sight being restored. How much more for us today when we activate and take the next step. Based on the spiritual principle of the healing at the pool of Siloam we should expect that we will see even more clearly.

As a side note, the pool of Siloam scripture highlights the joint foundational work of the apostles and the prophets (described in Ephesians 3:5 and 2:20) as apostles are the "sent" ones and prophets are meant to "see". Even if our major gifting is not the role or office of an apostle or a prophet then this scripture encourages us that we can still all walk in apostolic and prophetic gifting by this activation 1 exercise. This is because as we are 'sent' into our field of influence we will see more clearly (i.e. prophetic gifting); and by doing so we begin to lay down strong and healthy foundations for others to build upon (i.e. aspects of apostolic gifting).

Activation 2

Look at the areas of your life and ask God which of these is your sphere and which are not. Bring this principle into your daily diary. As a result, you may have to stop some things and re-start other things. Then give your YES to those things which are in your sphere of influence knowing that God will take care of the things outside of this. He is very good at his job.

Activation 3

Ask yourself, what is the land or the "dry bones" that are ready to hear you as you BENEDICT or speak Heaven's word of declaration and sound from your mouth to:

- unlock wells of previous revival (either spiritual, innovative or commercial)
- put flesh on the bones to restore, redeem and revive the mountains or culture shaping areas of influence in our society. These are: media, government, education, economy, family, religion, and arts and entertainment (as described by Lance Wallnau, 2013).

Chapter 9

A DICTIONARY OF DREAM SYMBOLS AND LANGUAGE

- Location (including buildings and contents)
- Colour
- Numbers
- Puns and wordplay
- Animals and creatures
- Transport
- People and parts of the human body
- Objects

Skill is acquired and revelation is given. Why start off this chapter with the statement I addressed in Chapter 2? The answer is simply to emphasize this key principle, particularly in the interpretation of dream symbols. Please remember, it is both about context (skill) and the spiritual help from God as "all interpretations belong to Him" (revelation).

The exhaustive list below is intended to be a help but not something to be relied upon in the absence of revelation. Otherwise we reduce the process of dream interpretation to a simple formula or a series of steps without spiritual significance and can potentially miss out on the unlocking of our destiny and purpose on the planet. We know that as we spend more time with a friend, we become more aware of the subtleties in their voice and tone. Similarly, as we spend more time with the God of Heaven, the creator of the universe and the lover of our soul then we will be able to go spiritually deeper and see an increased accuracy in our dream interpretations.

As all interpretations belong to God (Genesis 40:8), I and others have gone to the Bible to seek the interpretation of symbolic dream language. Many dreams occur throughout the Bible and it is full of many dream stories, allegories and metaphors to help people realise their destiny and life path. In this chapter I have put together a list of frequent dream symbols using various cross references, sources and expertise. This includes more than ten years of experience from the various live dream events hosted by our network (Speakers of Life) both in church environments, the general community (pubs etc..) and online events.

I have categorised these symbols into themes of everyday life, rather than simple alphabetical order, in order to help you remember them and for easy cross reference. Clarification of symbol meanings has also been cross referenced with the original language in the Bible together with other published lists written by John Paul Jackson, James Goll, Adam Thompson and Adrian Beale (see Chapter 10).

The length and aim of this chapter does not allow for a full list of names and their meaning. For this, please refer to the excellent dictionary of God's prophetic symbolism in everyday life by Adam Thompson and Adrian Beale (2011), and the *Prophet's Dictionary* by Paula Price (2006).

Location (including buildings and contents)

Before we notice any numbers or colours, dreams often begin with the dreamer being in a certain place, office, location or a room in a house. Some of these have been addressed in detail in Chapters 1 and 5.

House: your life (individual), family, business, a role or ministry, church, a personal life situation, home (2 Corinthians 5:1). Let's enter and go for a walk into the house and see what the rooms symbolise:

- **Front Porch/Verandah/Gateway**: Open, vision, exposed. Matthew 26:71.
- **Hallway**: transition, moving from one place of life or experience to another.
- **Kitchen:** a place of preparation including spiritual food. Here is an alphabetical list of examples of food symbols you might find in the kitchen and fridge in your dreams.
  - **Apples** can represent spiritual fruit or temptation, also something precious and valuable in the context of the apple of God's eyes (Psalm 17:8; Song of Songs 2:3; Proverbs 25:11; Genesis 3:6 (fruit of the tree)).
  - **Bread** represents Jesus Christ, the Word of God, the broken body or communion with God (breaking of bread), a source of nourishment and life. Manna or the bread of Heaven reflects God's miraculous provision coming directly from Heaven to sustain in a time of apparent lack. (John 6:35; Matthew 26:26-29; John 6:33-35; Exodus 16).
  - **Eggs** represent promise, new beginnings, a gift, something yet to be fulfilled i.e. not hatched yet or not yet realised. (Luke 11:12-13; Luke 24:49; Isaiah 59:5).
  - **Grapes** represent good fruit or fruitfulness, success in life, blood, fruit of the vine, being connected to Christ. (John 15:16, Genesis 49:11, Genesis 40:11).
  - **Honey** represents pleasant words, sweetness, abundance, flourishing, abiding, anointing, partaking of the best of the land. (2 Kings 18:32; Song of Songs 4:11; Deuteronomy 6:3; Jeremiah 11:5; Proverbs 5:3-4).
  - **Milk** represents nourishment, particularly for young or immature believers in the faith, foundational or elementary teaching. (1 Peter 2:2; 1 Corinthians 3,1-2; Hebrews 5:12-14).
  - **Water** (see also Chapter 5 for rivers and oceans). Holy Spirit, desire for God (thirsting), refreshing, Word of God, calm. (John 7;37-39; Ezekiel 32:14; John 4:14).
  - **Wine** in a positive context represents Holy Spirit, joy, a move

of God, blood. In a negative context it represents drunkenness. (Matthew 9:17; Genesis 49:11; Psalm 4:7; Ephesians 5:18; 1 Peter 4:3).

- **Dining Room/Table/Eating** represent nourishment (spiritual), fellowship (intimacy), (Revelation 3:20).
- **Windows** represent greater vision outside, but also symbolising the shedding of more light on an internal issue so you can see it more clearly.
- **Back porch** represents past issues of your life.
- **Garden** represents a place of intimacy with God (Genesis 3:8), intimacy, growth and fruitfulness (Numbers 24:6).
- **Basement** represents important foundational or basic issues which maybe hidden.

If there is more than one floor of the house, then it could represent multiple anointings. Let's go upstairs:

- **Elevator or staircase** represent rising (going up) or descending (going down) of gifting/anointing; or rising up to get a better/higher perspective; of coming up. (Revelation 4:1).
- **Bathroom** is a place of cleansing (see Chapter 5).
- **Bedroom** represents intimacy, union and rest. The bedroom in the physical realm is the place where decisions are often made as couples talk to each other at the end of the day. In 1995, my wife and I were looking around a particular house in the UK to buy but it had a price we could not afford. We were living in Paris at that time and I found myself on my own in the bedroom of the house we wanted to buy and I felt led to pray in that room as that would be the place where the sellers would decide on our offer. As a result, there was a dramatic shift in the mindset of the sellers. Not only did they sell the house to us at the price we could afford but in doing so they received incredible favour on their next house purchase, a true win win!
- The bedroom often has wardrobes for clothes and so here are a few items and their symbolism:

  - **Coat** represents a mantle/anointing.
  - **Pyjamas** represent spiritual slumber.
  - **Shoes** represent the path before you, authority on the land upon which you walk, gospel of peace.
  - **Swimwear** represents our ability to move in the Spirit; the Speedo style of swimwear represents increased speed.
  - **Wedding Dress** represents a deep relationship, commitment, covenant.
- **Attic** represents history that could be past (family) issues or spiritual gifts that had been given but which have not been used and are collecting dust.
- **Roof** represents covering and protection but also a new vantage point. (Genesis 19:8).

Common dream locations other than a house:

- **Office Building** can represent your daily work, but it could also be about getting things done with "your hands", as described for example in Deuteronomy 28. If it is a high-rise building, then it reflects the height of what you are called to do or achieve.
- **Hotel** represents a temporary place to relax or receive, passing through, may represent a night to receive revelation. (Genesis 28:11-15).
- **School, Classroom** represents a place of learning or training (See Chapters 1 and 3 for the birthing room beginning in the classroom dream). It could represent release of a teaching gift/anointing.
- **Shopping Mall** in a positive context represents provision for your needs all in one place under the same roof. As a negative, it represents self-centeredness.
- **Hospital** represents a healing place.
- **Theatre** represents either where your visibility will increase (i.e. if you are on the stage) or where you are going to see or be shown something (i.e. you are in the audience). An amphitheatre is

where all of this will be heightened or magnified.

- **Tent** represents temporary place of rest, human body, earthly dwelling place, meeting place with God. (2 Peter 1:13-14; Exodus 33:7-8).
- **Barn, Warehouse or Farm** represents storehouse of riches, harvest, provision (Malachi 3:10).
- **Petrol or Gas Station** represents a dedicated place not only to receive fuel and power but for it to happen quickly. An attendant may represent angelic help.
- **Theme Park** (e.g. Disney, Universal, Water park) in a positive context represents a place of adventure or extravagance (in God) or flowing in different aspects of the Holy Spirit (water park). In a negative context, it can represent a place of illusion or a failure to represent reality, deception which can lead to disillusionment.
- **Named City**. The name/meaning of city provides a wider context. For example, Atlanta links to a native American name which means "risen from the ashes", which is about rebuilding things that have looked lost or destroyed.

Colour

The next category that we are often aware of in a dream is colour. As with all dream symbols, the meaning depends upon the context so I have included all positive and negative connotations where appropriate.

- **Red** represents wisdom (this is often linked to the seven spirits of God in Isaiah 11:1-3), sacrifice, atonement, power anger, war, bloodshed. (Revelation 6:4; Revelation 12:3; 2 Kings 3:22).
- **Green** represents generosity, growth, life, hope prosperity, fruitfulness (linked to the fruits of the Holy Spirit described in Galatians 5:22-23), envy, jealousy. (Proverbs 14:30; Psalm 37:1-3).
- **Silver** represents the main meaning of redemption. For

example, Jesus was sold for silver to redeem humanity (Matthew 27:3-9) and in the wilderness the Israelites also offered silver for their redemption. The main point to highlight here is that as Jesus was the perfect redemption it ended the requirement for ongoing payment of silver for redemption. In this context, it is worth noting that there is no record in the Bible of silver in Heaven as we are already redeemed.

- **Gold** represents refining and the resulting purity, glory, holiness, wealth, anointing. (Zechariah 4:12-14; Revelation 3:18, 21:15-21, Malachi 3:3).
- **Blue** in the positive context represents revelation, communion with God, the colour of Heaven, Holy Spirit. Blue is often featured in the clothing of the priests and their elements in the temple. In the negative it represents depression, sorrow. (Numbers 15:38).
- **Purple** represents royalty (found in Royal gowns), authority, luxurious (Daniel 5:7; John 19:2; Judges 8:26).
- **White** represents righteousness, light (of the glory of God), purity, holiness, religious spirit, victory. (Revelation 19:8; Revelation 6:2; Mark 9:3).
- **Orange** represents perseverance, stubbornness, wisdom, glory (Ezekiel 1:4 and 27).
- **Brown** represents earthly (in contrast to Heavenly), compassion, humility, compromise. (2 Corinthians 4:7).
- **Black** represents death, calamity, mystery, sin. (Lamentations 4:8; Job 3:5).
- **Yellow** (linked closely to Gold) represents hope, Heavenly illumination, a lamp or light (Psalm 199:105), cowardice and fear (present day association).
- **Violet** represents foundational issues as the violet coloured precious stone of amethyst is the twelfth foundation stone in the New Jerusalem (Revelation 21:20); inheritance (linking back to foundations of generations).
- **Pink** represents being childlike, childish. (1 Samuel 17:42).

- **Grey** represents maturity, wisdom, loss of strength. (Genesis 42:38, Proverbs 16:31).

Numbers

This is another common category which occurs in our dreams, again the meaning depends upon the context and it's occurrence and usage in the Bible (this safe guards against going down the avenue of numerology). I have labelled a couple of numbers with an asterisk (*) which means that I have expanded the meaning of these numbers at the end of the number list.

1 God, foremost, beginning, source (John 10:30; Genesis 1:1).

2 Testimony, witness, multiplication or division depending on context (Matthew 18:16).

3 Godhead/Trinity (Triune God), resurrection (Matthew 12:40; Ezekiel 14:14-18).

4 Dominion (four corners of the earth), increased influence, expansion, world-wide (four directions of north, south, east and west and the winds from Heaven in Song of Songs 4:16), God's creative works (Genesis 2:10, Genesis 1:14-19).

5 Grace, favour, (1 Samuel 17:40, Genesis 1:20-23). See expansion below.

6 Man, flesh, Satan (Genesis 1:26-31; Numbers 35:15; 'Revelation 13:18).

7 Rest, complete perfection (Genesis 2:1-20 (rest on the 7th day of creation); Revelation 16:17; Joshua 6). The 7th day transfiguration (Matthew 17:1).

8 New beginnings (8 people came out of the ark to start anew), circumcision, (Genesis 17:12; 1 Peter 3:20). See expansion below.

9 Fruitfulness and gifts (there are nine fruits and gifts of the Holy Spirit), harvest, judgement (Matthew 27:45 (which mentions the ninth hour); Galatians 5:22-23; 1 Corinthians

12:8-10). It is interesting to note that the nine fruits of the Holy Spirit are described in Galatians 5:22 and adding 5+2+2=9 and Galatians is the ninth book in the New Testament.

10 Law, journey (Exodus 34:28).

11 Transition (between numbers 10 and 12), incompleteness (Genesis 32:22); taking from twelve or adding to what God has set out in ten.

12 Government, apostolic (Luke 6:12-13; Leviticus 24:5-6; Genesis 49:28 and Exodus 28:21).

13 Rebellion, adding to twelve, rebellion (Genesis 14:4; 16:12 and 17:25).

14 Double anointing of seven (Matthew 1:17).

15 Reprieve (Esther 9:20-22).

16 Established beginning (i.e. double new beginnings, eight).

18 Freedom from oppression. See expansion below.

24 Priesthood, governmental perfection (double 12). 24 elders around the throne of Heaven in Revelation 4.

30 Begin ministry, right time to reign (Genesis 41:46 and Luke 3:23).

40 Testing, humbling, dependence on God, wilderness before entering promise and time to reign, Deuteronomy 8:2; Acts 1:3, Matthew 2:6 and 4:2).

50 Jubilee, Pentecost (actually means 50), liberty and freedom (Leviticus 25:11; Acts 2:1).

100 Full harvest (Mark 4:20).

666 Lawlessness, Satan (Revelation 13:18, 2 Thessalonians 2).

888 Jesus, resurrection (based on the Hebrew "gematria" which is an alphanumeric code, assigning a numerical value to a name, word or phrase based on its letters).

***Expanded explanation of numbers**

(the additional meanings are underlined)

Number 5

Sometimes, the number 5 indicates recompense or bounteous reward. For example, thieves must repay 5 times the value of the oxen they steal (Exodus 22:1). Benjamin was honoured by his brother Joseph with 5 times more food than his other brothers (Genesis 43:34) and also with 5 sets of clothes (Genesis 45:22). A highlight of the number 5 is when Jesus took 5 loaves to feed 5 thousand; it was abundance for the multitude (Matthew 14:16-21, Genesis 1 20-23).

The number 5 also represents God's grace resulting in one blessing after another in our lives (John 1:16-17). It is also seen throughout the provision of the structure of the tabernacle for Israel whilst in the wilderness (Exodus 26 and 27):

- The pillars were 5 cubits apart and 5 cubits high.
- The brazen altar was 5 cubits by 5 cubits.
- There were 5 pillars at the end of the Holy Place.
- The sides of the tabernacle were reinforced by 5 bars on each side.
- The inner covering of the tabernacle was composed of 5 curtains which were attached to 5 other curtains for a total of ten curtains. Notice the double 5 pattern; doubling a number always indicates an abundance of the meaning.
- There were 5 original priests: Aaron and his four sons.

The holy anointing oil (Exodus 30:23-25), the ingredients of which were given directly by God, was used to consecrate the furniture of the tabernacle. It was comprised of five parts and as such represents a revelation of pure grace. The proportion of 4 spices used in making the oil were a multiple of five, which then had a hint of olive oil (5th element) added to it. These were pure Myrrh (500 shekels); sweet Cinnamon (250 shekels); sweet Calamus (250 shekels); Cassia (500 shekels)

Five also represents a number of preparations as detailed below:

- First 5 books of the Bible prepare you for Israel's story throughout the rest of the Bible.

- The 5 wise virgins were prepared with oil for their lamps (Matthew 25).
- David, in preparing to fight Goliath, took up five smooth stones from the stream as he ran to the battle line (1 Samuel 17:40).
- To prepare the saints for ministry, some are called to be one or more of the five-fold ministry of apostles, prophets, evangelists, pastors or teachers (Ephesians 4:11-12).

Number 8

The **new beginning** meaning of the number 8 can often be manifest as **pioneering,** representing change, challenging the status quo or a sign of **reformation**. Josiah, a pioneering reformer in the Bible, began his reign as King of Judah at the age of 8 (2 Kings 22 and 2 Chronicles 34). He also began to seek God as Lord of his life in the eighth year of his reign. Josiah's pioneering lead of a new era brought back the focus of the nation to following God. This was completely counter to the culture of his idolatrous predecessors.

One example of this was the purging of Israel from the altars of the false idol god, Baal. Likewise, King Solomon began to purge the idols from Israel in the eight year of his reign. King David was his father's (Jesse) eighth son and he ushered in a new era for Israel. The representation of reformation for the number 8 will always call us back to the straight path of flourishing life, the moral compass and righteous living taught by the Bible.

Number 18

This number has a strong link to **"Freedom" from oppression, bondage and captivity** and not simply a representation of oppression. The significance comes from the symbolic meaning of 18 for time periods or eras of bondage in the Bible.

After taking possession of the promised land, the children of

Israel were in bondage to several nations and peoples before Saul was eventually made king. For example, two of their enemies, Eglon the Moabite king and the Philistines (with the help of the people of Ammon) oppressed them for 18 years (Judges 3:12 and 14; Judges 10:7-8). After this time period, God raised up various Judges of Israel to deliver them from bondage and oppression. For example, the Israelites were freed from Eglon through Ehud being raised up to lead Israel (one of Israel's judges). God also raised up Jephthah in the East, and Samson in the South and West to free his people from the Ammonites and Philistines. Joshua, who led the children of Israel into the promised land after the death of Moses, was Israel's first Judge for the last 18 years of his life.

Interestingly this aspect of freedom from oppression is emphasized by the fact that there were 18 judges from the time of Joshua until Saul became king (1398 to 1050 BC). The 18 people who served as Judges were Joshua, Othniel, Ehud, Deborah, Barak, Eli, Gideon, Abimelech, Tola, Jephthah, Samson, Samuel, Ibzan, Jair, Elon, Abdon and Samuel's two sons Joel and Abiah.

Bondage and oppression can take many forms; it can be spiritual in nature. Jesus healed many demonically possessed or influenced people during his ministry. On one Sabbath, while teaching in a synagogue, Jesus healed a woman that had a 'spirit of infirmity' which had caused her to be bent over and crippled for 18 years (Luke 13:11).

Puns and Wordplay

There can be puns, wordplay or double definitions in dreams. The understanding of the meaning requires a subtle use of language that depends on spelling, sound, and definition. An expert in crossword puzzles will happily tell you this. Some examples in dreams are the following:

- The **Tail** of the part of the animal or creature versus a **Tale** of deceit or lies.
- A **Purpose** of intent or goal versus a **Porpoise,** an ocean dwelling mammal.

- The woman's name **Mary** versus **Merry** meaning joyful.

Sometimes the same word may have different meanings, such as writing on an item of clothing or a designer label. For example, I was leading a team in a Canadian shopping mall who were asking for prophetic clues from God in order to bless people. One of the clues was the word **Bench** which the team interpreted it as meaning a fashion label and so they walked up to a person with a **BENCH** shoulder bag and asked how they could pray and bless that person. Interestingly the meaning of the word 'Bench' to that person was that they needed to seek rest in their lifestyle to solve their headaches/ migraines. The word 'Bench' to them therefore meant lying down, a place where you are able to lie fully horizontal representing full rest.

Wordplays and puns occur many times in the Bible but sometimes the subtlety is lost in the translation process. Crossword solvers get ready!!! One example is read in the account of the prophet Amos. God shows him a basket of summer fruit which in Hebrew is *'qayis'* (Amos 8:1-3) and then, in response to Amos correctly identifying the fruit, God replies *"The end has come upon my people Israel…"* The word play here is that the Hebrew word for "end" is a similar sounding word "qes". The subtlety behind this is that God is saying the time was ripe for his people.

Another example is from Matthew 3:9 where Jesus says that, *"God is able to raise up children to Abraham from these stones"*. The Hebrew word play here is that the words for children/sons (ben), and stone (eben) are similar.

The account found in the book of the prophet Jeremiah is a very well-known example (Jeremiah 1:11-12). The two similar Hebrew words used here are *'shawkade'* (which means almond tree) and *'shawkad'* (which means "watch over my resulting word"). God asks Jeremiah what he sees. Jeremiah responds, *"I see the branch of an almond tree"*. God replies, *'You have seen correctly, for I am watching to see that my word is fulfilled.'* God uses the similarity of the words to encourage

Jeremiah that he is watching at all times to ensure that his word is fulfilled and does not return empty or unaccomplished.

The final two examples come from the Song of Songs which ultimately describes the divine romance of Jesus (the lover) with us (the beloved). The evocative nature of this divine romance is wonderfully captured by Song of Songs 1:3, which says of the lover *"your lovely name is flowing oil"* (this explains the dedication at the beginning of the book). As the Hebrew words for name and oil are *'shem'* and *'shemen'* respectively, the sentence would be read by an expert spiritual crossword solver as *"your lovely shem is flowing shemen"*. This reinforces the point that the name of the lover portrays his very nature.

The second example is in the same chapter, verse 2, which says: *"Let him smother me with kisses... I drink them in like the sweetest wine"* (TPT).

The Hebrew word for kisses and take a drink (wine) are very similar, suggesting that God's lovers will be drunk with love. The Hebrew word for kisses is 'nashaq' but it can also mean "to equip" or "to arm for battle". The deeper meaning is that the lovers of God need his kisses to become equipped like warriors to take on whatever the world throws at them, be it an army of hostility, people or adversity.

Animal and Creatures (alphabetical order)

It is worth mentioning that in a few cases, some of these relate to the modern day understanding of the animal that is then represented by the bible reference. In addition, some of those understandings for the purposes of dream interpretation will obviously relate differently in other cultures.

- **Alligator** (see Chapter 5).
- **Ants** represent irritation/unwanted guests, diligent, wise (Proverbs 6:6).
- **Bat** represents evil, unclean, fear (Leviticus 11:19).
- **Bear** (see Chapter 5).

- **Beaver** represents diligent, busy (Luke 10:42).
- **Butterfly** represents freedom, flighty, transformation (2 Corinthians 5:17).
- **Cat** represents witchcraft (black cat), independence, lazy, curious, vicious attack (Daniel 6:12, 24).
- **Cow** represents wealth ("cash cow"), subsistence, (Psalms 50:10).
- **Cockroach** (see Chapter 5).
- **Crocodiles** (see Chapter 5).
- **Deer** represent being sure-footed, spiritually sound, reaching new heights, thirsting after God (Psalm 42:1, Psalm 18:33).
- **Dog** (see Chapter 5).
- **Dove** represents Holy Spirit (Matthew 3:10)
- **Dragon** represents the devil (Revelation 12).
- **Eagle** represents prophetic (seer), calling, strength, lifted (by the Sprit). (Exodus 19:4; Psalm 103:5, Proverbs 30:19).
- **Fish** represent conversions (fish caught, souls of men), financial blessing (example of money in the fish's mouth (Matthew 17:27; Matthew 4:19).
- **Flies** represent evil spirits, Beelzebub means "Lord of the flies" and is a reference to the devil, living on dead things (Exodus 8:21-31, Matthew 12:24).
- **Fox** represents small sins that destroy fruitfulness, cunning, sly (Song of Songs 2:15; Luke 13;32).
- **Frog** represents an unclean spirit, (Exodus 8:2-13).
- **Hen** represents comfort, protects and gathers (Matthew 23:37).
- **Horse** represents power, strength but also death, warfare, famine (depending on the colour as described by the horses of the apocalypse in Revelation 6). (Revelation 9:19).
- **Lion** represents Jesus "Lion of the tribe of Judah"; royalty, brave, Satan prowling around looking to destroy (Revelation 5:5; 1 Peter 5:8; 2 Samuel 17:10).
- **Locusts** (also grasshoppers) represent devourer, numerous (Joel 2:25, Exodus 10:3-4).

- **Mice** (see Chapter 5), timidity.
- **Moths** represent destruction of valuable/treasured items, (James 5:2).
- **Oxen** represent strength (Proverbs 14:4).
- **Pig** represents unbelievers, unclean spirit (Matthew 7:6; Matthew 8:30-32).
- **Rat** (see Chapter 5), feeds on impurities in lives.
- **Scorpion** represents evil spirits, demonic power, harsh discipline, stinging words (Luke 11:12; Revelation 9:5).
- **Sheep, Ram** represent the people of God, innocent, vulnerable; humility, submission, sacrifice.
- **Snake** (see Chapter 5), can also represent deception, lies, gossip (Genesis 3:4; Psalm 58:4).
- **Sparrow** represents small value but precious (Matthew 10:29-31).
- **Spider** (see Chapter 5), can also represent witchcraft, being tangled (Job 8:14, Isaiah 59:5).
- **Wolf** represents Satan, predatory, false, deception (John 10:12; Genesis 49:27: Matthew 10:16).

Transport

This section is quite brief as it is covered in more detail in Chapter 1. In general, the larger the vehicle then the larger the influence, calling or ministry in your life.

- **Airplane** represents travel, moving to new heights (in the Spirit i.e. a prophetic seer gifting); higher profile (this can relate to a business, corporation, church). The size, make and company flying the plane will correlate to the interpretation (Isaiah 40:31; Acts 8:39).
- **Armoured Vehicle** represents protection of your calling (by God).
- **Bicycle** represents individual ministry or destiny which

is self-propelled (it can represent doing things in your own strength), no horsepower thereby requiring perseverance.

- **Bus** represents church or ministry as there is a body of people with a driver.
- **Car** (compared to a bus or airplane) symbolizes personal ministry, your life and destiny. A convertible car or soft top represents an open Heaven or thin place to Heaven.
- **Fire Truck or Engine** (UK) represents extinguishing fires of damage or destruction, enables the rescue of a situation or people.
- **Limousine** represents a high profile, being taken (chauffeur) to your destiny in style.
- **Motorcycle** represents fast, responsive manoeuverable, powerful and independent ministry.
- **Ocean Liner or Cruise Ship** represents a journey or voyage impacting a large number of people.
- **Sailing Boats/Windsurfers** represent powered by wind of the Spirit, scale denotes whether it is personal (windsurfer) or you are bringing people with you (yacht).
- **Speedboat** represents accelerating destiny or ministry, power of the Holy Spirit.
- **Submarine** represents not openly shown or observed, undercover, can be representative of underground Church in oppressive countries.
- **Subway (train)** represents undercover and active, a way of getting from one place to another without being seen or engaging with busy traffic (i.e. people or danger).
- **Taxicab** (if the passenger) represents paying a price to get to the place where you are going; (if the driver) represents a business opportunity to your destiny; can mean being driven by money.
- **Train** represents nothing gets in the way, a powerful large movement of God that is difficult to stop.
- **Tractor** represents strength (slow power) and can often

parallel the oxen symbolism, preparing for harvest, sowing, breaking new ground.

- **Truck or Lorry (UK)** represents ability to deliver, large ministry.

People and Parts of the Human Body

The right hand or right side of the body symbolizes that which has been added or acquired over your life such as skills etc. In addition, it can also mean long life, greater blessing, salvation, authority, honour (preferred pre-eminence), strength, double portion (Proverbs 3:16; Genesis 48:17-19; Psalm 110:1; Colossians 3:1). For more on this please refer to the teaching by John Paul Jackson (Chapter 10).

The left hand or left sidedness can represent that which you have been born with such as skills, abilities (see John Paul Jackson teaching). Left can also symbolise foolishness, judgement (goats), unusual strategy or direction, riches and honour or weakness (of man) which actually emphasizes God's strength and ability to be the solution to the weakness (Ecclesiastes 10:2; Matthew 25:33,41; Judges 3:20-21; 2 Corinthians 12:9-10; Proverbs 3:16).

- **Baby** represents a promise (of God), new ministry, responsibility, beginning or idea, jumping ahead of God's timing (premature baby) dependent, helpless, innocent, trying to make it happen (induced labour) (Acts 7:5, Hebrews 5:12-13; Revelation 12:2-4).
- Twins represent double blessing/anointing or double trouble. Pregnancy represents the process of reproducing, preparatory stage, the promise of God, the Word of God as seed, anticipation and expectancy.
- **Miscarriage** is to lose something at the preparatory stage, whether good or bad, plans aborted.
- **Beard** represents maturity (Psalms 133:2), removal of a beard can represent being cleaned up/ being made ready, depending on the context (see Joseph needing to be shaved in Genesis 41:14).

- **Bride** represents Christ's church, covenant or relationship. (Ephesians 5:25 and 31-32: Genesis 2:24).
- **Hair** represents wisdom and anointing (Proverbs 16:31).
- **Lawyer** represents an advocate, mediator or representative in a court room (Jesus Christ acts as an advocate); legalism such as the accuser in a court room (Satan). (1 John 2:1; Revelation 12:10).
- **Policemen** represent Spiritual authority for good or evil; protector.
- **Prisoner** represents captive, a lost soul, oppression, addiction. (Timothy 2:26; Ephesians 4:1; Isaiah 61:1).
- **Teeth** represents wisdom, maturity, words, comprehension, understanding. Eye teeth symbolise revelatory understanding or a seer gifting. Wisdom teeth is simply the ability to act in increased wisdom compared to those around you. (Psalm 35:16; Hebrews 5:14).
- **Nakedness** represents seeing the person as they really are, transparency, humility, shame, feeling vulnerable (Hebrews 4:13; Revelation 3:17; Genesis 3:7 and 10).
- **Neck** represents strength or support, stiff necked, stubborn, proud, subjection, victory (foot on neck). (Psalm 133:1-2, Job 41:22, Isaiah 31:6, Psalm 75:5, Isaiah 48:4).

Objects

- **Knife** represents a brutal attack, form of protection, severing (a person who causes division), cutting. (Judges 19:29; Isaiah 54:17).
- **Sword** represents the Word of God, far reaching in terms of the application of the cutting, double-edged, divides and separates, words, authority (Ephesians 6:17; Revelation 1:16; Revelation 2:12; Psalm 55:21, Revelation 19:15).
- **Gun** represents spiritual authority, spiritual attack or threatening words (loaded gun); or fake threats intended for

intimidation represented by a gun full of blanks or a toy replica gun that has no power. A gun filled with water represents the impartation or shooting of the Holy Spirit's power to bless and not destroy (Isaiah 54:17; Psalm 22:13).

- **Dart** represents curses, demonic attack, fiery darts. A positive symbolism is accuracy, always hitting the target like a dart board (Ephesians 6:16; 2 Samuel 18:14; Proverbs 7:23).
- **Arrow** represents a positive symbolism in the form of the blessing of children, negative symbolism is accusation, piercing words (Psalm 127:4-5; Proverbs 25:18; Deuteronomy 32:23).
- **Shield** represents faith, protection, God's truth, faith in God (2 Samuel 22:3; Psalm 18:2; Ephesians 6:16-17).
- **Key** represents spiritual authority, opening and closing of doors that represent opportunities and timing (Isaiah 22:22; Revelation 9:1, Matthew 16:19).
- **Television** represents spiritual sight and understanding, message, entertainment, fleshly desires, letting the world in, reception (Numbers 24:4; Numbers 12:6).

Drenched in Heaven's rain

Chapter 10

PRAYERS AND RESOURCES

- I Want to Give My Life to Jesus (prayer)
- Bibliography and Recommended Books
- Recommended Teaching and Online Resources
- How to Connect

I WANT TO GIVE MY LIFE TO JESUS

The prayer does not have to be complicated; it is as easy as ABCD:

A. **A**dmit you have been living your life your way and not God's way and you have been running away from God. *"All have sinned and come short of the glory of God"* (Romans 3:23).

B. **B**elieve that Jesus is the son of God and he died on the cross for your sins and rose from the dead. *"Believe on the Lord Jesus Christ, and you will be saved"* (Acts 16:31). *"God demonstrates his own love for us in this: while we were still sinners, Christ died for us"* (Romans 5:8).

C. **C**onfess and repent of your sins, in other words say sorry to God and turn around and run back to God, and receive God's forgiveness. *"If we confess our sins, he is faithful and just to forgive our sins"* (1 John 1:9).

D. Decide to accept Jesus as your loving Lord and Saviour, in other words invite him into your life, as if inviting him into your car which symbolises your life. Give him the driving seat and give him permission to drive your car, giving him the steering wheel of your life; then declare that Jesus is the driver and he can take you wherever he likes. "*If you declare with your mouth, 'Jesus is Lord,' and believe in your heart that God raised him from the dead, you will be saved. For it is with your heart that you believe and are justified, and it is with your mouth that you profess your faith and are saved*" (Romans 10:9-10).

Bibliography and Recommended Books

Abley, Steve. *The Return of the Musical Prophet: Understanding the transforming power of music and sound.* River Publishing and Media Ltd, 2014.

Addison, Doug. *Understand Your Dreams Now: spiritual dream interpretation.* eGenCo publishers, 2013.

Birch-Machin, Mark. *Speakers of Life: How to live an everyday prophetic lifestyle.* River Publishing and Media Ltd, 2014.

Brewer, Troy A. *Numbers that Preach: Understanding God's Mathematical Lingo.* Aventine Press, 2007.

Empson, J. *Sleep and dreaming.* 3rd edition. New York: Palgrave/St. Martin's Press, 2002.

Goll, Jim. *The Seer: The prophetic power of Visions, Dreams and Open Heavens.* Destiny Image Publishers, 2005.

Goll, James and Michal Ann. *Dream Language: The prophetic power of dreams, revelations and the spirit of wisdom.* Destiny Image Publishers, 2006.

Gotink R. A., P.C. Chu, J. V. Busschbach, H. Benson, G. L. Fricchione, Myriam Hunink MG. "Standardised Mindfulness-Based Interventions in Healthcare: An Overview of Systematic Reviews and Meta-Analyses of RCTs." *PLOS One* 10, No. 4, 2015.

Henderson, Robert. *Operating in the Courts of Heaven.* Robert Henderson Publishers, 2014.

Hobson, J.A. "REM sleep and dreaming: towards a theory of proto-consciousness." *Nature Reviews Neuroscience* 10, No. 11: 803–813, 2009.

Hooper, Francis John Bodfield. *Palmoni: An Essay of the Chronological and Numerical Systems in Use Among the Ancient Jews*. Longman, Brown, Green, and Longmans, 1851.

Hutchison, Isabel C. and Shailendra Rathore. "The role of REM sleep theta activity in emotional memory." *Front Psychol* 6: 1439, 2015.

King, Patricia. *God's Law of Attraction: Revealing the Mystery and Benefits of Your Soul's Prosperity*. XP Publishing, 2015.

Leaf, Caroline PhD.*Switch On Your Brain: The Key To Peak Happiness, Thinking, And Health*. Baker Books, 2013.

McCraty, Rollin, Dana Tomasino. "Modulation of DNA conformation by Heart-focused Intention." Institute of HeartMath. *Psychology*, 2003.

Mahan, Milo. *Palmoni; or The Numerals of Scripture a Proof of inspiration*. (1863) Reprint, BiblioBazaar, 2009.

Markov, Dmitri, Marina Goldman, Karl Doghramji. "Normal Sleep and Circadian Rhythms: Neurobiological Mechanisms Underlying Sleep and Wakefulness." *Sleep Medicine Clinics* 7, No.3, September 2012.

Montijn, Ronald. *Courts of Heaven for Beginners: A practical guide for presenting your case in the courts of Heaven*. Seraph Creative, 2019.

Price, Paula A. *The Prophet's Dictionary: The ultimate guide to supernatural wisdom*. Whitaker House, 2006.

Rob, Alice. *Why we Dream*. Picador publishers, 2018.

Springer, Rebecca Ruter. *My Dream of Heaven*. (Intra Muros 1898). Reprint, White Crow Books, 2010.

Stark, Emma. *The Prophetic Warrior*. Destiny Image, 2020.

Takeuchi, Tomoka. "Dream mechanisms: Is REM sleep indispensable for dreaming?." *Sleep & Biological Rhythms* 3, No. 2: 56–63, 2005.

Takeuchi, T., A. Miyasita, M. Inugami, Y. Yamamoto. "Intrinsic dreams are not produced without REM sleep mechanisms: evidence through elicitation of sleep onset REM periods." *Journal of Sleep Research* 10, No.1: 43–52, 2001.

Thompson, Adam and Adrian Beale. *Divinity Code to Understanding Your Dreams And Visions*. Destiny Image, 2011.

Thompson, Adam and Adrian Beale et al. *God's prophetic symbolism in everyday life*. Destiny Image, 2017.

Wallnau, Lance and Bill Johnson. *Invading Babylon: The 7 Mountain Mandate*. Destiny Image Publishers, 2013.

Recommended Teaching and Online Resources

Mark Birch-Machin. "Working from REST."
https://soundcloud.com/thebaychurch/mark-birch-machin-7
Delivered on 18th November 2018 – Heavenly Encounters 9.

Speakers of Life YouTube channel: Dream interpretation teaching, recorded workshops and examples
https://www.youtube.com/c/SpeakersofLife

Leif Hetland. "The Three Chairs."
https://www.youtube.com/watch?v=Ulpx06Xg7Fo

John Paul Jackson and Stream Ministries
http://www.streamsministries.com

- Basics of Dreams, Visions and Strange Events– John Paul Jackson
- The Biblical Model of Dream Interpretation – John Paul Jackson
- Prophets and Psychics – John Paul Jackson
- Understanding Dreams and Visions – John Paul Jackson

Doug Addison Ministries.
http://dougaddison.com

- The Dream Crash Course

Mark Virkler and Charity Kayembe, "Hearing God through your dreams." XP media.
https://wisdom.xpmedia.com/p/hearing-god-through-your-dreams

Emma and David Stark, Glasgow Prophetic Centre.
https://www.propheticscots.com/

British Isles Council of Prophets.
https://www.prophets.org.uk/

Robert Henderson Ministries.
http://www.roberthenderson.org/

Rebecca King and Invictus Prophetic Network.
https://www.facebook.com/RebeccaKing29/

James Goll and Network Ministries.
http://encountersnetwork.com/index.html

Julia Powell. "Just Believe Prophetic Art."
www.just-believe.co.uk

How to connect with Mark Birch-Machin

and the Speakers of Life (SOL) network

SOL is a Christian prophetic network and a UK Community Interest Company (number 12074412)

e-mail: enquiries@speakersoflife.org
website: www.speakersoflife.org

Facebook: www.facebook.com/speakersoflife
YouTube channel: https://www.youtube.com/c/SpeakersofLife

* 9 7 8 1 9 0 8 1 5 4 5 4 5 *

BV - #0026 - 211122 - C0 - 229/152/10 - PB - 9781908154545 - Gloss Lamination